DERIVATIVES
in a DAY

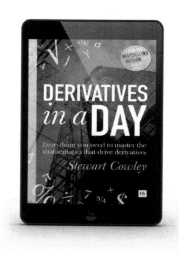

DERIVATIVES
in a DAY

Everything you need to master the
mathematics powering derivatives

Stewart Cowley

Hh

HARRIMAN HOUSE LTD
18 College Street
Petersfield
Hampshire
GU31 4AD
GREAT BRITAIN
Tel: +44 (0)1730 233870

Email: enquiries@harriman-house.com
Website: www.harriman-house.com

First published in Great Britain in 2019.

Paperback ISBN: 978-0-85719-637-8
eBook ISBN: 978-0-85719-638-5

British Library Cataloguing in Publication Data
A CIP catalogue record for this book can be obtained from the British Library.

ABOUT THE AUTHOR

Stewart Cowley has been working in the financial markets since 1987. He is one of a handful of people ever to have held a triple-A rating by Standard & Poor's and was awarded the prestigious Gold Medal for long-term investment performance by FE Trustnet. He has also been one of the UK's most visible fund managers, having written for the *New Statesman*, the *Sunday Telegraph* and *Citywire*. He has made frequent appearances on the BBC and Sky News. His previous books *Man Vs Money* and *Man Vs Big Data* have both been bestsellers.

"And what there is to conquer
By strength and submission, has already been discovered,
Once or twice, or several times, by [those] one cannot hope
To emulate – but there is no competition –
… For us, there is only the trying"

– From 'East Coker', *Four Quartets*, T. S. Eliot

CONTENTS

1. INTRODUCTION

In his 2003 annual letter to Berkshire Hathaway shareholders,[1] the money-managing goliath Warren Buffett called derivatives "financial weapons of mass destruction". Many people, even those who didn't know what derivatives were, nodded in agreement – and those who nodded most vigorously knew the least about derivatives. That's because derivatives – financial instruments deriving their value, not from owning something, but from the price movements of something they are related to (like stocks, bonds, currencies and commodities) – are both fiendishly simple and fiendishly difficult to understand.

Or so a lot of people would like you to think.

These prejudices have some basis in truth: derivatives nearly single-handedly brought about the near-collapse of the entire Western financial system in 2008. But, besides this trifling incident, it is arguable derivatives have been given something of a bad rap. This is understandable if you perceive them to be complex and anarchic, but also if the sheer size of derivatives markets turns your knees into quivering jellies.

---

[1]   www.berkshirehathaway.com/letters/2002pdf.pdf

To give you a sense of perspective, if you were to project all the money and financial assets in the world onto the side of the 102-floor Empire State Building, the first 81 floors would be the derivatives markets. The next 13 floors would be occupied by global debt markets; five floors would be reserved for global stock markets; the remaining floors by actual cash in circulation, gold and real estate. The small blinking red light on the top of the communications tower would be Bitcoin.[2]

As of December 2016, the Bank of International Settlements – the financial organisation owned by 60 member states which act as the central banks' central bank – calculated that there were derivatives with a notional value of $500 trillion swilling around the world, with profits of $15trn sitting inside the instruments falling under its governance. Fifteen trillion dollars is close to the value of the total annual national income of the United States, a truly staggering number.[3,4] From the late 1990s, until its near-term peak in 2013, the derivatives market achieved an astonishing 15% compound annual growth rate, making it one of the true growth industries of the modern era.

---

2   *Man Vs Money*, p.175.

3   www.bis.org/publ/otc_hy1705.htm

4   US GDP is about $18trn. tradingeconomics.com/united-states/gdp

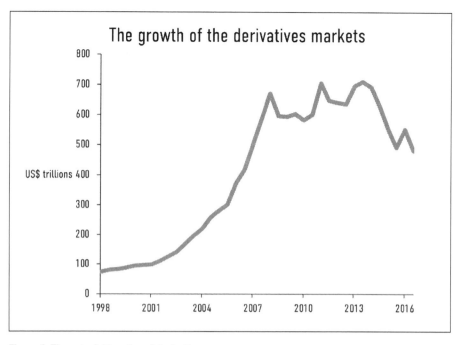

Figure 1: The astonishing rise of derivatives

Suspicion surrounding the derivatives market isn't helped by a lack of transparency. Although derivatives can be traded on regulated exchanges, making oversight easy, there also exists an over-the-counter (OTC) market where derivatives are traded between private institutions. Here, timely visibility of the market structure and its risks are all but impossible.

For many, this opacity, and the nervousness that comes with it, masks the fundamental usefulness of derivatives, especially if you are an administrator or risk manager. But the competitiveness of fund management means fund managers no longer have the luxury of being able to allow investment strategies to work themselves out over months or years; they need to be able to react and trade quickly, and the place to do that is the derivatives market. League tables of fund performance, published on a daily basis, expose fund managers to the kind of minute scrutiny more normally reserved for football or baseball managers. It's a poisonous cocktail of rational behaviour and irrational expectations.

Fortunately, modern portfolio management has moved on in the past few years, in all kinds of ways. We now have a myriad of new mechanisms to defend our clients' money from the ravages of market volatility and the unexpected. This is only right as we face a whole new set of threats and opportunities in the interconnected world of global finance.

This is where derivatives can help.

For those of you not blessed with the mathematical abilities of most people who work in the derivatives markets – the sort of talent enabling you to calculate large prime numbers in your head, for instance – I promise to keep this book as simple and straightforward as possible. This is for pedagogic reasons, but also because I have noticed that, as I get older, my ability to handle higher mathematics has diminished somewhat. I also believe the mathematics of derivatives obscures their basic usefulness. Derivatives really are intensely practical things and, if you can pick out the principles behind them, there are things so mind-bogglingly useful inside of them you start to wonder why you hadn't done this kind of thing before.

There are lots of basic ideas and some important practical day-to-day questions I want to answer in this book, which can be boiled down to:

1. What are derivatives?

2. How do I alter the characteristics of a portfolio using derivatives?

3. How do I protect a portfolio using derivatives?

4. How do I increase the returns to a portfolio using derivatives?

5. Why do shoe repairers sell sports trophies?

The following chapters address these questions, although I suspect question five will evade the reasoning of even the most enquiring mind. But every one of these problems can be managed using a derivative of some sort. To aid the process, I will use simple spreadsheet examples with all the workings revealed so that you can create and play with these ideas at your leisure. Also, where I can, I will include relevant Bloomberg screens and internet resources to show you how systems can help you, although I accept that private investors and college students may not have the $2,000 per month it costs to have Bloomberg terminal installed on their computer. Still, for those working in fund management companies, it might help you find your way around the backwaters of a system some have taken an entire career to understand.

This book is also written with as much humour and anecdotal illustration as can be mustered from a musty subject. You will discover possibly the most disastrous national collaboration the world has ever seen. You will also come to understand how Thales of Miletus, in 350BC Greece, only missed having red braces, a large cigar and a New York accent by 2,400 years. But you shouldn't mistake a light touch for a lack of serious intent. As someone who worked in the financial markets for 30 years (please feel free to jump in at this point and exclaim "No! Really, Stewart! You don't look old enough!"), this is also a heartfelt and practical manifesto on the more obvious opportunities, and even mistakes, made for and by derivatives users.

I dare say there are more learned and detailed texts you could buy. My aim is to push you in the right direction rather than drop you onto a pinhead from 30,000 feet. Still, this book may feel a little didactic at times – especially when I use words like 'didactic' – but I want to give you the benefit of hard-won lessons and experience. Treat this as your diving board for the leap into a much bigger subject.

If you follow the step-wise process outlined here, this time tomorrow you could be bragging about being able to perform delta hedging on your portfolio to your co-workers at the water cooler. Exciting, isn't it!

2. THE ORIGINS OF DERIVATIVES: WHERE ITALY AND JAPAN COLLIDE

Derivatives aren't new. The first organised use of derivatives was on the Dojima Rice Exchange in Japan around 1700, providing two places to buy and sell rice: the *shomai* and the *choami*. The shomai market allowed merchants to buy and sell grades of rice at today's price (the so-called **spot price**). But the real fun took place on the choami market. 'Choami' roughly translates as 'rice trading on books'; traders could buy and sell standardised agreements for a set amount of rice at a pre-arranged price on a specified settlement date. These were legal **contracts**. No contract could carry over to the next settlement period and all profits and losses had to be made good, in cash, by handing over the difference between the price of rice on the settlement day and the price written on the contract.

No rice changed hands – the value of the contracts was *derived* from the underlying price movement between the day the contract was made and the day it was settled. The contract would be worth money to the owner if the contracted price was below the spot price on the day of settlement (in theory they could buy it from the person on the other side of the contract and then immediately sell it in the market for a profit).

The system worked so well that the market functioned without much interruption until 1937 – nearly 250 years. But for the whole thing to work required the inventiveness of another nation, Italy.

What the Japanese harnessed was the genius of a Florentine mercantile agent called Francesco Balducci Pegolotti. Pegolotti wrote *The Practice of Commerce* in about 1340 showing, for the first time, tables of interest on a loan stretching over many years. This allowed lenders and borrowers a hitherto unprecedented level of precision in their dealings with each other. More importantly, it enabled the calculation of what you should pay for something in the future, as long as you knew its price today and the cost of borrowing money. Today, we know Pegolotti's mathematical formula as the **compound interest equation** – one of the civilisation-shaping equations of which very few people understand the importance.

You are about to join a very select group of people.

2.1 ALL PRESENT AND ACCOUNTED FOR

Pegolotti, the Italian banking dynasty that was the Medici, and everyone who has followed them in finance, have enjoyed whole lifetimes of employment based upon the understanding and manipulation of this simple equation:

$$FV = PV(1+r)^n$$

Equation 1

Contained within this equation is the ability to work out the **future value** (FV) of an investment whose **present value** (PV) is known and invested at a rate (r) for a number of years (n). It also offers the ability to earn mind-boggling bonuses in the financial markets, if you know how to use it, and is the destroyer of worlds if you don't. More importantly, it sits at the base of the derivatives markets.

Bringing together the stylish Italians and the precise Japanese hasn't always worked – the Alpha Romeo Arna (the acronym stands for Alfa Romeo Nissan Autoveicoli) was voted the worst Italian car of all time[5] – but when it came to derivatives it created the largest financial market the world has ever seen.

Understanding the compound interest equation is important so it's worth going through some examples.

Let's imagine it is 1983 and you aim to be one of only 26,000 people to buy the calamitous Alpha Romeo Arna which, at the time, cost about $5,000.[6] The anxious-looking dealer has offered a 'buy now, pay later' deal of $5,300; you pay no money for a year but you get to limp around in your Arna (when the electrics work). In 1983, interest rates were about 10% per annum.[7] What is the fair price of the car? Using our compound interest equation we can work this out.

If you placed the $5,000 on deposit at your bank and earned interest in the meantime, after a year you would have:

$$\text{Future value} = 5{,}000 \times (1 + 0.1)^1$$
$$= \$5{,}500$$

You will achieve an effective discount of $200 if you accept the terms of the 'buy now, pay later' offer (the $5,500 you earn from the money in the bank compared to the $5,300 required to settle the deal). If the

5   www.telegraph.co.uk/cars/gallery/the-10-worst-italian-cars-ever/alfa-romeo-arna

6   www.classicandperformancecar.com/alfa-romeo/arna/3865/1983-1987-alfa-romeo-arna

7   www.bankofengland.co.uk/boeapps/iadb/Repo.asp

car dealer had access to Pegolotti's equation, he could have marked up the price by $200, to take away your advantage, or he could just leave it as an incentive for you to buy.

So, taking time into account, and the opportunities on both sides of the transaction, you have just priced your first derivative. In fact, you've just priced a **forward contract** – a contractual obligation to purchase something at a fixed price at a fixed point in time in the future. The agreed price is called the **delivery price**, also known as the **forward price**, and the day when the agreement ceases is called the **delivery date**. As the buyer (and owner) of the contract, you are deemed to be **long**. As the seller of the contract, the car dealer is **short**.[8]

Fundamentally, that's it – all financial derivatives start here. Pretty much anything else you will learn about derivatives is simply complication piled upon complication of this basic principle. I recommend that you make sure you understand it before progressing.

2.2 DAY-COUNT CONVENTIONS: MONKEYS EAT BANANAS UPSIDE DOWN

Eating a banana, you might think, is pretty straightforward. But opinion is divided. The process starts with stripping away the skin to reveal the off-white flesh of what is technically a berry. This, all creatures are agreed upon. What we are not agreed upon is which end of the banana to start from. We homo sapiens start from the end formerly attached to the herbaceous plant. Monkeys start from the other end. Nobody knows why – the monkeys may know something

---

8   You may have heard the phrase "And that's the long and the short of it" meaning here are both sides of the story; nothing is complete without understanding the winner and the loser.

we don't, or it could just be a meaningless difference. Either way, it's a good illustration of a principle: no matter how simple a task is, someone will find a different way of doing it.

This is a good thing to remember when working with financial calculations – a realm of both maddening complexity and maddening oversimplification, where there can be 31 days in February and 365 days in a leap year.

Let's take a forward contract. From the specifics of the contract, we know today's date in days, months and the year $(D_1/M_1/Y_1)$ and we know the delivery date $(D_2/M_2/Y_2)$. Subtracting one from the other should enable us to count the number of days remaining. However, there are four conventions for doing this in general use, as listed in figure 2.

Day-count basis	Convention
Actual/Actual	Actual days elapsed between two dates/annualised number of days between dates
Actual/365	Actual days elapsed since last date/365
30/360	If D1 = 31 then D1 = 30 If D1 = D2 = 31 then D2 = 30 If D1 = 31 & D2 = 30 then D2 = 30 else D2 = 31
30E/360	If D1 = 31 then D1 = 30 If D2 = 31 then D2 = 30

Figure 2: The most common day-count conventions

For simplicity, we are going to use the 30/360-day method throughout this book because it is so common; 30 days in a month and 360 days in a year.

2.3 FORWARD AND EVER ONWARD! PRICING A SIMPLE FORWARD CONTRACT

You can perform the fair value, compound interest calculation by hand if you wish, but it's much easier to put it into a spreadsheet:

	A	B			A	B
1	Value	5,000		1	Value	5000
2	Time(days)	360		2	Time(days)	360
3	Interest Rate	10.00%		3	Interest Rate	0.1
4	Future Value	5,500		4	Future Value	=B1*(1+(B3*B2/360))
5	Saving	500		5	Saving	=B4-B1
6				6		
7				7		

Figure 3: A simple spreadsheet to calculate a forward contract value

You might like to have a play around with the numbers at this point, changing the amounts, interest rates and time. Someone may even mistake it for actual work. Finished? OK – let's start moving things around in a more systematic way and see what happens to the fair value calculation. Imagine you drive your brand new Arna home, and there on the six o'clock news is a headline saying:

'Alpha Romeo Arna has catastrophic fault!!! Dealers slash prices!!!'

A quick scan of trade magazines (the internet hasn't been invented yet) shows your brand-new car has dropped in value to $4,000 (put this into cell B1 in the spreadsheet). An identical 'buy now, pay later deal' is now worth $4,400 and yet you are locked in to paying $5,500 in a year's time. If you wanted to get out of your legal obligation to the dealer today, you would have to pay them $1,100 (the difference between what you agreed to pay the dealer and what the car is now worth). Ouch!

Now, in a parallel universe, let's imagine you come home to this unlikely headline instead:

'Alpha Romeo Arna voted best car of all time!!! Mad panic as customers rush to buy!!!'

A scan of trade magazines shows the amazing popularity of the Arna (we really are in the world of fantasy now); prices have risen to $6,000 and the 'buy now, pay later' deal will cost $6,600. To get out of the contract, the dealer would have to pay *you* $1,100.

There is an easy lesson here. **After a contract has been established, as the (spot) price of any commodity inevitably moves up or down, someone is going to win and someone is going to lose**. The contract will vary in value throughout its life until, one day, at the settlement date, everybody has to divvy up and go their separate ways.

Now let's imagine that the length of your 'buy now, pay later' deal is still one year but, this time, interest rates move while the spot price is unchanged. Let's say interest rates rise to 12% in an instant (not an uncommon event in the 1970s). What is the contract worth now (plug 12% into cell B3 of your spreadsheet)?

$$\text{Future value} = 5{,}000 \times (1 + 0.12)^1$$
$$= \$5{,}600$$

So, in this case, keeping your money on deposit for a year would gain you an advantage of $300 over the agreed $5,300. Drop interest rates to 8% and the contract would be worth $5,400 meaning that, when it came to delivery, you would have to find an extra $100 to settle the contract.

You might like to try one final experiment. Change the time value to 1 (day). Now change the interest rate and/or the spot rate. What you should notice is that, try as you might, it is very difficult to get the forward rate to differ from the spot rate in any meaningful way.

This is an important principle: **a forward contract becomes less volatile as time passes and the forward rate converges towards today's spot rate**.

So, forward contracts are not static things; they rise and fall in value in between the day they are created and the day they finish. Time, interest rates and prices are the nemesis of certainty in the world of the forward contract which can be a good thing and a bad thing. In the world of finance, any moving price can be traded, which creates markets and allows opinions and preferences to be expressed. It makes the world go round.

2.4   I'M A FORWARD CONTRACT – GET ME OUT OF HERE!

Not many forward contracts ever get to their delivery date; they are negated at some point, either by the person who realises they have got it terribly wrong and want to cut their losses, or by the person who has made a profit and wants to cash in at what they think is the optimum moment. You would imagine all parties could come to an agreement, albeit reluctantly on one part, hand over some cash and forget about the whole sorry affair – until next time.

How it actually works is somewhat different. The contract can't be cancelled (it exists in law); instead it is negated by creating an equal but opposite transaction to cancel it out. Imagine this situation: you bought the disastrous Arna for $5,300 on 31 May for delivery on 31 May the following year, but on 14 June you realise the contract is worth $5,600. If there was a ready market for such things you could sell an Arna to the dealer for the prevailing market price of your contract matching the delivery date in the process. In accounting terms it would look like this:

Date	Delivery date	You	Amount	Dealer	Amount
31 May 2018	31 May 2019	Buy	5,300	Sell	5,300
14 June 2018	31 May 2019	Sell	5,600	Buy	5,600
Total			300		-300

Figure 4: Cancelling out a forward contract with an equal but opposite contract

Creating an identical but opposite transaction crystallises the profit or loss long before the delivery date. After that, no matter how much market prices or interest rates move around, the profit and loss is locked in. Actual money changes hands when the contract expires.

Being able to cancel out contracts, by creating an equal but opposite position, hands you the opportunity to trade the volatility of the underlying 'thing' – be it a car, a financial market or a commodity. It also allows you to speculate on future price movement. You don't even have to own the underlying thing; just the desire to trade or a view of how its price will move in the future. This is why forward contracts are *so* popular for pure speculation, and explains why the Japanese rice traders established the choami market over three hundred years ago.

Speculators love forward contracts for another reason: you don't have to put any money down to play the markets. You do need to establish with your counter-party that you will be good for any losses occurring which, under most circumstances, will be a fraction of the notional value being played with. You could, for instance, have $100,000 in the bank, take out a forward contract for $3,000,000 and make $10,000 in a matter of minutes. This would equate to an absolute 10% return on your money. The converse can also happen and you lose 10%. But the idea of ratcheting up your investments compared to your available capital – in this case 30 times (3,000,000/100,000 = 30) – is just too tempting for some and has a name: **leverage**.

The ability to use leverage through forward contracts and other derivatives to create preternatural returns, is in no small way responsible for the creation and growth of something called the **hedge fund industry** – an area of high risk and, hopefully, high returns which uses leverage in abundance. According to data gathered by Barclay Hedge, the money managed by hedge funds rose from just $118bn in 1997 to over $3trn towards the end of 2017.[9] It's a success story Francesco Balducci Pegolotti would have been proud of.

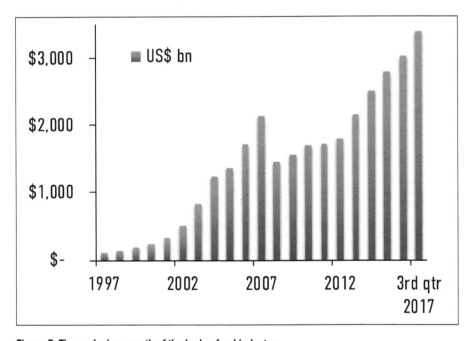

Figure 5: The explosive growth of the hedge fund industry

---

9   www.barclayhedge.com/research/indices/ghs/mum/Hedge_Fund.html

2.5 CONCLUSION

The scales should have just fallen from your eyes about how the world really works. This is a good thing. At least from the point of view of understanding the rest of this book.

This chapter should have taught you the following features of forward contracts:

1. You receive delivery of your item at a specified date in the future.

2. You could have the money on deposit.

3. The price you pay in the future is dependent upon today's price, and the interest rate, until the delivery date.

4. If interest rates or the price of your item moves in the interim, someone is going to experience a profit or loss.

If you have recreated the spreadsheet shown in this chapter (which I strongly suggest you do), have a play around with it to make sure you understand what can happen to forward contracts when things start moving around, and as time passes. It's an important set of concepts to get into your head and key to the successful use of derivatives during your career.

3. FUTURES BASICS: MY FUTURE'S SO BRIGHT I HAVE TO WEAR SHADES

W e use derivatives pretty much every day; we just don't know it. But anywhere you buy something today and promise to pay for it sometime in the future, you are using a derivative. Credit cards, service agreements, buying your dream kitchen on an 'install now, pay later' basis – they are all derivatives of a kind.

In this chapter we are going to look at how the ideas developed in chapter 1 are used in the financial markets. There is no better place to start the next leg of our journey than the simplest one of all – the place where people exchange the money of one country for the money of another country, the foreign exchange markets.

3.1 JUST ONE MASSIVE BUREAU DE CHANGE

According to the Bank of International Settlements (BIS), the amount of foreign exchange traded each day is about $5trn,[10] of which about $3trn involves forward contracts in one way or another. It's a truly impressive amount of money, dwarfing all other financial markets. But, in the process of being bamboozled by the sheer size of the

---

10   www.bis.org/publ/rpfx16.htm

numbers, you shouldn't lose sight of the fact that it is just one massive bureau de change like the ones you find in any airport.

Like an airport bureau de change, all transactions in the foreign exchange markets consist of selling one currency (the US dollar, Japanese yen, euro etc.) and buying another. Buying the Alpha Romeo Arna in the last chapter only involved one interest rate – the interest earned on your cash in the bank during the forward contract. When we exchange currencies there is an interest rate on *both sides* of the transaction to be accounted for; both the buyer and the seller have money which could be on deposit.

If you are buying another currency, if you had it today, you could put it on deposit at the rate applicable to that currency. The same is equally true for the seller on the other side of the transaction; they are foregoing interest they could have earned. For the world to be in equilibrium, **interest rate parity** must be maintained – i.e., the interest you are forgoing, by not receiving your new currency today, has to be paid for. This is done by adjusting the forward price up or down, such that nobody is losing out.

To see how this works, let's use an example. You are selling US dollars one year forward. One-year US interest rates are 4%. You are buying Japanese yen where one-year interest rates are 0.5%. The current exchange rate for purchasing Japanese yen/US dollar (the spot rate) is ¥115 per US dollar. What should the forward rate be to make the two situations equal? From interest rate parity we know that for every dollar owned and every yen yet to be owned, after one year of being on deposit, their value will be:

$$\$1 \times (1 + 4\%) = ¥115 \times (1 + 0.5\%)$$

So,

$$\$1 = 115 \times 1.005/1.04$$
$$\$1 = 115 \times 0.9663$$
$$= 111.13$$

Forward rate adjustment = 111.13 - 115 = -3.87 points

Note that currency price movements and differences are measured in points and fractions of a point are called **pips**.

So, you now get less yen for your US dollars, i.e., they are more expensive. Why? Your counterparty is forgoing 4% of interest for a year while you are forgoing a measly 0.5%. The interest rate difference is reflected in the forward price; your yen/US dollar rate is adjusted to compensate the seller of yen for the interest they aren't receiving. More generally, the equation to work out the forward price is:

$$\text{Forward rate} = \text{Spot rate} \times (1 + R_{buy})/(1 + R_{sell})$$

Equation 2

There is a more accurate and technically correct way of doing this, which we'll come to later, but for the time being you should get used to the idea of interest rate parity mainly because there is a whole career as a foreign exchange dealer summed up in this section. Some of these dealers are driving around the City of London in Ferraris with number plates like FX 1 just for understanding it.

If you were to put this calculation into a spreadsheet, it would look like this:

	A	B	C
1		Buy	Sell
2		JPY	USD
3	Spot FX Rate	115.00	
4	Interest Rate	0.5%	4.0%
5	Delivery (Days)	360	
6	Years	1.00	
7	Forward Rate	111.13	
8			

	A	B	C
1		Buy	Sell
2		JPY	USD
3	Spot FX Rate	115	
4	Interest Rate	0.005	0.04
5	Delivery (Days)	360	
6	Years	=B5/360	
7	Forward Rate	=B3*(1+B4*B6)/(1+C4*B6)	
8			

Figure 6: Pricing a forward foreign exchange contract

If you are moving from a low interest rate to a higher one, the situation is reversed (see below) and the forward price is revised upwards to compensate the other side of the trade.

	A	B	C
1		Buy	Sell
2		USD	JPY
3	Spot FX Rate	115.00	
4	Interest Rate	4.0%	0.5%
5	Delivery (Days)	360	
6	Years	1.00	
7	Forward Rate	119.00	

Figure 7: Pricing a forward contract going from a high to a low interest rate

In general the rule is:

• when going from a low interest rate to a higher interest rate, the forward price decreases

• when going from a high interest rate to a lower interest rate, the forward price rises.

Whenever you do this calculation, all you need to know is the spot rate and the interest rates on both sides of the trade coinciding with the settlement date. This date is important because the interest rate differential is rarely constant – the interest rate differential depends upon the delivery date; the difference between one-month interest rates is usually different to three-month differentials; three-month differentials are different to six-month's, and so on (see illustration below). In general, the longer you put money on deposit the more interest you receive (hence the upwards sloping plot of deposit rate against time) but this isn't a hard rule. However, the interest rate differential isn't the same along the time axis and, therefore, the forward price will be different depending on the delivery date you choose. Every calculation has to be done individually in the foreign exchange markets.[11]

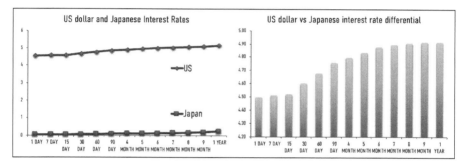

Figure 8: Interest rate differentials aren't constant along the yield curve

Forward foreign exchange contracts have many uses. Most commonly they are used for **hedging** – reducing unwanted foreign exchange risks on assets you own. Foreign exchange hedging is used by portfolio managers as well as buyers and sellers of goods in the real economy. For instance, imagine you are a US-based manufacturer and you know you have to hand over ten million euros in six months' time. In the interim, you could leave yourself at the whim of the foreign exchange markets as they fluctuate on a daily basis; you could pay more or, if

---

11   These curves are based upon the London Inter-bank Offered Rate (LIBOR) which for many years has been the standard for pricing financial products. However, due to a series of scandals surrounding the rate-setting procedures it is set to die out. At the time of writing this book it is not known what the new deposit rate benchmark will be (there may be several) so we'll just talk in the vaguest possible terms about short-term interest rates.

you get lucky, less for your euros. To take out the uncertainty, you could buy the euros at today's price (adjusted by the interest rate differential) for delivery in six months' time. You are now locked into a fixed euro/ US dollar rate.

Similarly, investment portfolio managers holding the stocks or bonds of foreign companies and governments expose their investors to wanted or, sometimes, unwanted foreign exchange risks compared to the base currency of the portfolio. To eradicate the currency risk for strategic reasons, the fund manager could hedge the foreign exchange exposure back into the base currency of the portfolio. They could do this either for a specified length of time (say three months) or, continuously, by 'closing out' the forward before the delivery date (creating an equal and opposite transaction after say two months) and establishing a new forward contract with a more distant date. This is called **rolling the forward**. Graphically, it looks like this:

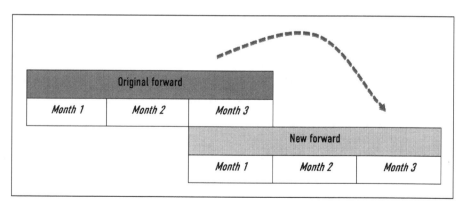

Figure 9: Rolling a three-month forward contract after two months

Rolling forward contracts before they expire is very common in the foreign exchange markets but it also allows another activity – speculation. Because an investor puts no money down to establish a forward foreign exchange contract (they merely create a legally binding agreement to do something at a fixed time in the future and at a fixed price), they can play the leverage game described in chapter 2 to their heart's content. Hedge funds and other speculators love the foreign exchange markets for this reason.

3.2 BACK TO THE FUTURE…

Forward contracts are agreements struck privately between consenting adults. They are bespoke, infinitely flexible but ultimately non-standard; they are the Savile Row tailoring of the financial markets. They are sometimes called **over-the-counter** (OTC) derivatives. You carry the risk that your counterparty may go bust in-between the initial trade date and the delivery date. If you are a speculator, and your counterparty reneges or defaults on their obligation, you won't get the money you are owed. If you are using the forward contract as a hedge, the situation is even worse. You now have an unhedged position exposing you to a risk that you had hoped to neutralise. Counterparty risk is a very real and dangerous phenomenon.

This is where the **futures markets** come in. Financial futures are standardised contracts traded on an exchange. These can be physical places although, increasingly, trading is done electronically. Here, your counterparty risk is with the exchange itself, or a centralised clearing house (a kind or administrative go-between), which does all the administration for you. It takes in an initial payment (called **margin**) to cover possible losses, works out the profit and loss from your derivatives position, and moves money around between the winners and losers each day. It's a fine system. The largest exchange for derivatives in the world is the CME Group incorporating the Chicago Mercantile Exchange, the Chicago Board of Trade (CBOT), the New York Mercantile Exchange (NYMEX) and the Commodity Exchange (COMEX). In 2017, over four billion contracts traded there.[12] Its nearest rival was the National Stock Exchange of India with two and half billion trades.

The 'cost' of eliminating counterparty risks is that financial futures contracts lack the flexibility of a bespoke forward agreement. Futures contracts are of a fixed size rather than an infinitely variable amount. You could sell $1,201,864.65 forward into the euro, for instance, using an OTC forward contract whereas a futures contract is worth a fixed amount, commonly $100,000 of the underlying commodity. To cover $1,200,000 (rounding the previous example) you would have to buy or sell 12 contracts (1,200,000/100,000). But this is a minor inconvenience compared to the other advantages.

Futures contracts also have a rigid set of delivery dates; usually the end of each quarter year, but there are monthly futures contracts on some commodities. Defining your settlement date as 14 October at your whim just doesn't exist in the world of futures. Here is a summary of the characteristics of futures and forward agreements so you can see for yourself the relative advantages and disadvantages.

---

12   www.statista.com/statistics/272832/largest-international-futures-exchanges-by-number-of-contracts-traded

Feature	Forward agreement	Futures contract	Advantage/disadvantage
Delivery date	Anything you like	Fixed to specific 'active' month or quarter year-end dates	Forwards are more flexible but, unless you are doing very fancy things, the more approximate futures dates are good enough for most purposes.
Size	Anything you like	Each contract has a fixed size	Forwards are hidden from the market while futures are seen through the open dealings in the market (creating greater transparency and better oversight).
Counterparty risk	The other side of the contract could go bust	Spread out among lots of people on the exchange	There is a small price to be paid for the risk-spreading process – exchanges need money to run them. But this is a small price to pay given the alternative.
Pricing	Has to be calculated from known characteristics each day by the broker/ yourself	Published in newspapers and on information systems in real-time	If maintaining positions on computer systems, it is obviously easier to get a price feed for futures than having to calculate things by hand (requiring lots of inputs).

Figure 10: Futures contracts vs forward agreements

The global futures market is truly impressive. Its sheer size, and the breadth of things bought and sold, covers just about anything you could reasonably want, and a couple of things you shouldn't have. Everything from entire stock markets, currencies, bonds, gold, oil, metals, coffee and – my own personal favorite – lean hogs, is ready to be bought and sold. All you need is an account with a futures broker and away you go.

Trading futures is so easy and ubiquitous that the total outstanding value of all the derivatives in the world is now eight times bigger than the global income, as measured by global gross domestic product.[13] And the innovation to increase the size of the futures markets hasn't really slowed down much. An army of (mainly) young people spending their most vibrant years thinking up new and ever more sophisticated ways of applying the principles of the futures markets to increasingly bizarre situations. In 2003, the world came within a hair's breadth of seeing the first ever 'terrorism future' – investors could, effectively, bet on the probability of a terrorist attack. The idea was that information would leak out about an imminent attack and someone, somewhere, would seek to protect themselves from it. The more probable an attack became, the more the price of the future rose. So the theory went. This derivative was created not by a cynical Wall Street derivatives firm but by the United States Pentagon. The justification given was that the US intelligence organisation could more perfectly gather information using market pricing than having people running around the world in rain coats and dark glasses. It was later withdrawn as being "distasteful".[14] Fortunately, the internet and big data has stepped in to take its place, and now you can be watched 24 hours a day via your phone without the need for a market mechanism to gauge whether or not a terrorist attack is imminent. **But the lesson is clear: if there is a risk out there, perceived or real, someone will create a derivative for you. All you have to do is ask**.

---

13 'Liquidity Pyramid', *Independent Research*, 10 March 2006.

14 hanson.gmu.edu/PAM/press2/FRQ-Sum-04.pdf

3.3 PRICING A STOCK INDEX OR ANY OTHER FUTURE

To show you the flexibility of futures contracts, let's go even bigger – how about a whole stock market? To price a future on a stock market, we use all the same elements: money on deposit; the price (the index level); and an interest rate you are forgoing (dividend yield of the index).

Using the same approach as interest rate parity, where we put the index 'on deposit' and expect the index future plus dividends to provide the same return, the price of a stock index future will look like this:

> Index × (1 + Deposit rate) = Index futures price × (1 + Dividend yield)

Equation 3

> Index futures price = Index × (1 + Deposit rate) / (1 + Dividend yield)

Equation 4

Let's lay this out in a spreadsheet and price a three-month (0.25 of a year) stock index future. The index is trading at 2,700 and has a dividend yield of 1.7% while the three-month deposit rate is 3%. The only difference here from our currency example is that we are using a fraction of a year (3/12 months), so we have to adjust our annualised interest rates by taking a quarter of their value:

	A	B
1	Index Level (Spot)	2,700.00
2	Time (Years)	0.25
3	Deposit Rate (annualised)	1.70%
4	Dividend Yield (annualised)	3.00%
5	Interest Rate Difference (annualised)	-1.30%
6	Future Rate	2,691.29
7	Discount/Premium (Index Points)	(8.71)
8	Percentage Difference	-0.32%

	A	
1	Index Level (Spot)	2700
2	Time (Years)	0.25
3	Deposit Rate (annualised)	0.017
4	Dividend Yield (annualised)	0.03
5	Interest Rate Difference (annualised)	=B3-B4
6	Future Rate	=B1*(1+(B3*B2
7	Discount/Premium (Index Points)	=B6-B1
8	Percentage Difference	=B7/B6

Figure 11: Pricing an equity market future

The stock index future price can be expressed in the equivalent number of index points (cell B7) which is -8.71 points, in this example, because deposit rates are higher than the dividend yield. The calculated futures rate is also known as the **fair value** of the futures contract. It is the *theoretical* fair value of the future, not the value of the future you might see in the market. The market value of any future may fluctuate above and below the fair value. The difference between the fair value and the market value – called the **basis** – is a function of sentiment, supply and demand, and other market conditions. Price discrepancies above and below fair value are the food arbitrageurs feed upon; if a future is trading very far away from its fair value price (the basis is abnormally low or high), arbitrageurs will buy undervalued contracts, or sell overvalued contracts, to return it back close to the fair value price, banking the profits in the process.

It must be said that there are a number of different equations for the theoretical value of a futures price. For instance, Chicago Mercantile Exchange uses this version in its literature:[15]

Fair value = Cash (1 + r(x/360)) – Dividends

Equation 5

Where:

---

15   www.cmegroup.com/trading/equity-index/fairvalue.html

Cash = Index level

r = Deposit rate

Dividends = Dividends due by the expiration of the contract expressed in index points

The other, more technically correct, equation to calculate the fair value of a futures contract uses compounding which occurs every day. This is the **continuous compounding equation**:[16]

$$\text{Futures price} = Se^{(r - q)(T - t)}$$

Equation 6

Where:

S = Spot index level

e = Euler's number approximately equal to 2.71828

r = Deposit rate

q = Dividend yield

T – t = Time between now and delivery date

If we use the numbers from our previous example and plug them into both methods using a spreadsheet, you can see they give very similar results. The difference is accounted for by rounding the effects of continuous compounding. The function e is represented by the =EXP( ) function in spreadsheets while the ^ symbol takes care of the need to raise Euler's number to the power of (r - q)(T - t).

---

16   *Options, Futures and Other Derivative Securities* by John Hull, p.44, Prentice-Hall International Editions.

	A	B
1	Index Level (Spot)	2,700.00
2	Time (Years)	0.25
3	Deposit Rate (annualised)	3.00%
4	Dividend Yield (annualised)	1.40%
5	Interest Rate Difference (annualised)	1.60%
6	Future Rate	2,710.76
7	Discount/Premium (Index Points)	10.76
8	Percentage Difference	0.40%
9		
10	CME approach	2710.80
11		10.80
12		0.40%
13		
14	Using continuous compounding	2,710.82
15		10.82
16		0.40%

	A	B
1	Index Level (Spot)	2700
2	Time (Years)	=90/360
3	Deposit Rate (annualised)	0.03
4	Dividend Yield (annualised)	0.014
5	Interest Rate Difference (annualised)	=B3-B4
6	Future Rate	=B1*(1+(B3*B2))/(1+B4*B2)
7	Discount/Premium (Index Points)	=B6-B1
8	Percentage Difference	=B7/B6
9		
10	CME approach	=B1*(1+B3*B2)-(B4*B1*B2)
11		=B10-B1
12		=B11/B10
13		
14	Using continuous compounding	=B1*EXP(B5*B2)
15		=B14-B1
16		=B15/B14

Figure 12: Comparing different approaches to pricing equity index futures

As time goes by, the futures price converges to the spot price to such an extent that, on the date and time of expiration, the futures price and the spot stock index price are the same; the basis becomes zero. The $(T - t)$ part of the equation has done its work as it trundles towards zero.

Easy isn't it? In fact, it's so easy you should try and think of other types of situations you could apply it to: bonds, oil, gold, concentrated orange juice, pork bellies, anything really. Each has its own variations inside of it, like accounting for the cost of storing commodities, but the essence of the calculation is the same.

With a small adaptation (the inclusion of a negative sign just after Euler's number), the continuous compounding equation turns into another very important equation:

$$PV = Se^{-(r - q)(T - t)}$$

Equation 7

This **continuous discounting equation** enables us to find the present value of something offered in the future. It's the opposite of the continuous compounding equation. We'll be seeing a lot of these two equations going forward.

3.4 CONCLUSION

Our sun has been gently throbbing away, giving light and warmth to our planet, for about five billion years. This has, in turn, produced:

- life

- conscious thought

- human beings

- social groups

- advanced mathematics, science, literature and art.

But, one day, our sun will start to lose its vigour. The mass at the centre of it will stop pulling in the gaseous outer layer and it will begin to expand. As it expands, it will envelop the solar system and boil our earth into a small black cinder revolving slowly in space forever. You could say we have about five billion years to get out of town.

Between then and now, I can confidently predict that financial markets will go up and down. In fact, I will go further: I confidently predict that derivatives on the price of water will be invented, and an unscrupulous group of investors will try and corner the market shortly before the vast puddle we know as the Pacific Ocean evaporates. When pricing their water future, those same investors will use nothing more complicated than what we have been talking about in this chapter.[17]

---

17   The settlement date will have to be set carefully so as to be just before final extinction of life.

To summarise this chapter:

1. Futures trade on exchanges to eliminate counterparty risk.

2. Futures trade in fixed amounts for fixed delivery dates.

3. You could have the money on deposit, and/or are forgoing income in the meantime, which means you have to adjust the spot price up or down by way of compensation.

Once you have these three principles in your head, everything else pretty much follows. I recommend you go back over the spreadsheet examples and play with the numbers – just to get the feel for things. It will be worth it.

4. OPTIONS BASICS: WHAT ARE MY OPTIONS HERE?

Thales of Miletus did a steady trade in the sort of pithy quotes you find on posters on the walls of university undergraduates: 'The most difficult thing in life is to know thyself', 'Avoid doing what you would blame others for doing' or 'Nothing is stronger than necessity'. As one of the Seven Sages of Ancient Greece he was a veritable one-man cottage industry of quotable quotes.

Thales was also one of the original 'maths geeks' and, in an act of calculated gambling, he made a fortune snapping up the right to use olive presses just before a particularly strong harvest. If the harvest came in as abundantly as he expected, olive growers would be climbing over themselves to get to him and his access to the presses. The value of his rights of usage would skyrocket. If the harvest failed, or was mediocre, his rights would expire worthless.

The key word here is **right**. Not to actually do something, or promise to do something, but the *right* to do something if the circumstances were advantageous. Unknowingly, Thales of Miletus had invented a derivative we know as an **option**. If Thales had been alive today, he would probably be wearing red braces while shouting at people in a New York accent.

A financial option is simply the right to buy or sell something at a specific time and price. You aren't obliged to do anything; you can exercise your rights, or not, depending on whether it is to your advantage. For this privilege, you lay out a fraction of the total cost but it won't be catastrophic if you lose it (unless it's all the money you have, of course).

It's a simple idea but it didn't really catch on for a long time. A chequered history in the US during the 1920s meant the general public was wary of options. Even the Chicago Board of Trade (CBOT), which held a license to develop the options market as a regulated and standardised exchange, resisted the temptation until the 1960s, when the Chicago Board Options Exchange (CBOE) established open-outcry trading pits, similar to those at its affiliated futures exchange, along with centralised clearance and settlement. Even then it took a bit of mathematical wizardry, which Thales of Miletus would have approved of, to really get things going because nobody had answered the question as to what the 'correct' price was for an option. The solution to option pricing will soon become clear but first, just so that everybody is on a level playing field, let's make sure you understand the language of options.

4.1   WELL, STRIKE ME DOWN!

Finance is littered with bewildering words. After a while, you start to suspect most financial language was specifically designed to keep the tourists away, in the same way that assistants in computer shops will want to ridicule you over your lack of understanding of PCMCIA slots. Frankly, it took me years to scratch the surface of the meaning of some of the following because they have nothing but a passing relationship with conventional modern usage. I have a sneaking suspicion that options must have been around in Elizabethan England, and here's why.

There are two types of options – **calls** and **puts**. A call option is your right to *buy* something. A put option is your right to *sell* something.

You have to have some kind of arcane internal dialogue to get the hang of these terms. It runs like this:

> "Sire, I **call** upon you to sell this pig to me, as was our agreement."

Or:

> "Sire, it is my understanding that I can **put** this pig to you, as was our agreement."

Either way, you sort of end up standing in your best doublet and hose, hands on hips, legs somewhat apart, bouncing up and down at the knees, pronouncing like a Shakespearian actor at the Globe Theatre. Which can be somewhat embarrassing when everybody around you is dressed in powder blue shirts and off-white chinos.

But it gets even worse. Instead of saying an option has ended, we say it has **expired**. Expiring is the sort of thing ladies did in Elizabethan times because of diseases now treatable with aspirin. Option contracts have specific expiration dates – they last for a fixed time. So, our examples above become:

> "Sire, I call upon you to sell this pig to me on this, the **expiration** day, as was our agreement."

or

> "Sire, it is my understanding that I can put this pig to you on this, the **expiration** day, as was our agreement."

Now things are going to get even more weird. Not only do we have the option to buy or sell something on a specific day, we also have a specific price to do it at. This is called the **strike price** as in to 'strike a bargain'. Our porky example now becomes:

> "Sire, I call upon you to sell this pig to me at the price we did **strike** the bargain, 100 groats, on this, the expiration day, as was our agreement."

Or:

> "Sire, it is my understanding that I can put this pig to you at the price we did **strike** the bargain, 100 groats, on this, the expiration day, as was our agreement."

The final complication is that the option market doesn't always talk about the price of an option. It is interchangeably called the **premium**.

Here is a table summarising these basic terms. There really isn't anything more complicated here than agreeing to buy or sell something at a specific price on a specific day.

Option language	Meaning
Call	Buy
Put	Sell
Strike	Price of an option
Expiration date	Date when you may buy/sell at the strike price
Premium	Price of an option

Figure 13: The mysterious language of options demystified

During the rest of this chapter, I'll keep defining these terms just to hammer home their meaning – it takes a while to get used to them.

4.2   JOLLY HOCKEY STICKS

If we plot how the value of a call option (right to buy) or a put option (right to sell) changes as the price of the underlying commodity changes, it looks something like a hockey stick. To understand how this shape is derived, imagine a stock called Thales of Miletus PLC possessing put and call options trading on it, with strike prices of $65. Thales of Miletus PLC stock is currently trading at $50.

A call option on the stock with a strike price of $65 is essentially worthless; you could buy the stock in the market cheaper. As the stock price rises and exceeds the $65 strike price, the call option suddenly becomes valuable. The call option is said to possess **intrinsic value**.

Intrinsic value of a call option = Market price - Strike price

As the Thales of Miletus PLC stock rises further so too does the value of the call option; at $67 the call option is worth $2 ($67 market price - $65 strike price). This process continues into infinity as the stock price rises.

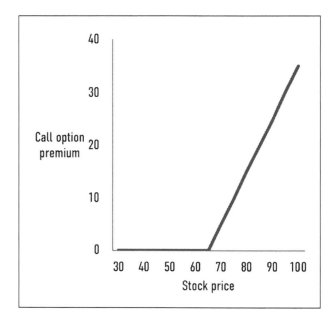

Figure 14: The value of a call option

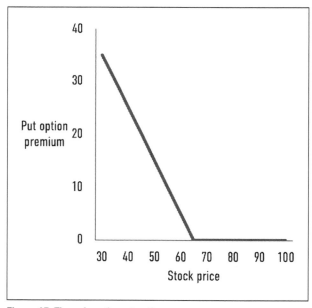

Figure 15: The value of a put option

Now let's imagine Thales of Miletus PLC is trading at $80 and the stock price begins to fall. At this time, a put option on the stock is essentially worthless: you could sell the stock in the market for a price higher than the strike price. And it remains worthless until the stock of Thales of Miletus PLC hits the $65 strike price and keeps falling. The value of the put now begins to rise:

Intrinsic value of a put option = Strike price - Market price

Equation 8

When the value of Thales of Miletus PLC falls to $63, the put option would have an intrinsic value of $2 ($65 strike price - $63 market price). The value of the put option keeps rising until the stock price hits $0. The value of a stock cannot fall below zero so the maximum value the put option can ever achieve is $65.

The behaviour of options, as the stock price rise and falls, can be represented graphically as a **pay-off diagram**.

4.3 THEM VERSUS US: AMERICAN AND EUROPEAN OPTIONS

Nothing really tells us more about the difference between Europeans and Americans than the way we approach the same task. The more mundane the task, the greater the differences between us, it seems. Take, for instance, the exercising of an option. You would have thought it was simple: the clock ticks by and when the option hits the expiration time on the expiration date, it disappears in a cloud of legal language and you either exercise your rights or not.

Sadly, this is not the case. If you think of Europeans as rigid bureaucrats, with a penchant for administrative rigour, and Americans as more casual, free-finance gunslingers, then you have the difference between European and American-style option exercising:

- European-style options expire on a specific day, at a specific time, and can only be exercised at that moment.

- American-style options also expire on a specific day, at a specific time, but can be exercised any time before expiration – all you have to do is say when.

Obviously, there is greater uncertainty as to when an American-style option is going to be exercised, which has to be modelled and allowed for in the price. For this reason alone, an American-style option, although possessing admirable flexibility, will cost at least the same as an equivalent European-style option. For our purposes, we are going to stick with European-style options because they make the calculations simpler to perform and explain.

4.4 WE'RE IN THE MONEY, WE'RE IN THE MONEY[18]

There are three states a professional fund manager exists in: expecting a bonus, receiving a bonus and being disappointed by a bonus. Similarly, there are three basic states an option can exist in and they are defined by the relationship of the underlying commodity price to the strike price of the option. If the stock price is the same as the strike price then it is said to be **at-the-money** (ATM). Imagine now that the market price of the stock is below the strike price of a call option. The option isn't worth much – has no intrinsic value – and so is said to be **out-of-the money** (OTM). If the market price is above the strike price then the option has intrinsic value and is said to be **in-the-money** (ITM). The converse is true for put options: stock price below strike price, in-the-money; stock price above the strike price, out-of-the-money. These states are summarised in the following table.

---

18   'We're in the Money' lyrics by Al Dubin, music by Harry Warren (from the film *Gold Diggers*, 1933).

Call option		
Relationship	Option state	Intrinsic value
Stock price = Strike	At-the-money	0
Stock price > Strike	In-the-money	> 0
Stock price < Strike	Out-of-the-money	0

Put option		
Relationship	Option state	Intrinsic value
Stock price = Strike	At-the-money	0
Stock price > Strike	Out-of-the-money	0
Stock price < Strike	In-the-money	> 0

Figure 16: Option pricing in a nutshell

In practical terms, you will find the price (premium) of an option is greater than its intrinsic value. There is a good reason for this: right up to the moment of expiration, there is a *chance*, no matter how vanishingly small, that the final stock price could be the right side of the strike price to make the option valuable, and for this there is a price. As such:

Option price = Intrinsic value + Time value

So an option two points in-the-money may trade at a price of 2.5 points with 0.5 points of time value. The longer the time to expiration, the greater the time value. But, as time passes, the time value gradually becomes eroded, and the option premium declines even if the underlying asset doesn't move in price. The option price will fall to the intrinsic value (if it has any) at expiration. If the option has no intrinsic value, the value of the option will fall to zero at expiration. This gradual erosion of value illustrates why you really shouldn't hold on to options for too long; there will always be an optimum time to sell your options, and move onto the next (longer-dated) contract, before the ravages of time start to have their way.

The time value of options has important practical consequences. Investors don't always buy at-the-money options. Sometimes they may wish to purchase out-of-the-money options for reasons of cost; a very out-of-the-money option will be considerably cheaper than an at-the-money option, and they will get a greater bang for their buck if the stock price moves. They will have bought more options for the same monetary outlay. For instance, an at-the-money call option may cost 2.5 points but, using a higher strike price, an out-of-the-money call may trade at just 0.5 points. So, for the same money, you could get five times more options (2.5/0.5) which will pay out more if there is a radical movement upwards of the underlying commodity price. It's another route to attaining the evil and terrible leverage discussed in previous chapters, but with none of the downside risks besides the loss of your original premium.

4.5 CONCLUSION

Options have a bewildering language of their own. No matter the words, they are rooted in some simple ideas. Like any new skill, once you get the hang of them you'll be wondering what all the fuss was about.

- A call is a right to buy.

- A put is a right to sell.

- The strike is the price you may buy or sell at.

- The expiration date is the day your rights cease to exist.

5. PRICING OPTIONS: RIEN DE PLUS — NO MORE BETS PLEASE

What Thales of Miletus had actually done was buy a call option on olive press usage. He had bet on there being a bumper harvest and that, consequently, the value of his call option would rise. Whenever you enter the realm of betting you are also entering the realm of probability and statistics. Thales more than likely had an inkling of this when he said, "The past is certain, the future obscure".

But how do you come to the 'correct' price for an option? How can you include this obscure future into an equation to value a financial instrument? The world had to wait 2,320 years to get close to the answer. In a breathtaking leap of imagination, Fischer Black and Myron Scholes formally wrote out what many had been approximating through guess work – a theoretical framework for the price of an option. They applied their work to the markets and promptly lost their proverbial shirts. Undeterred, and with three years' more work, aided by the contribution of Robert C. Merton, the version of the equation now known as the **Black-Scholes-Merton model** (BSM) was published in 1973. It revolutionised the derivatives market and, in 1997, Scholes and Merton received the Nobel Prize for their work. (Black missed out on the award having died, aged just 57, in

1995. The Swedish Academy did at least give him a mention during the ceremony.)

We'll get to the detail of the BSM model in time but first let's understand the concepts involved.

5.1 OPTION PRICING: THE EASY WAY TO THINK ABOUT IT

Let's imagine you are definitely going to buy a stock at some point in the future. For the time being, we are going to ignore dividends.

To price an option you have to have two concepts in your mind.

First, what is the probability that, in a couple of months, the stock price will be the same as the prevailing stock price (S)? It could be higher, lower or the same. Let's call this probability P(S).

Secondly, what is the probability that, in a couple of months, the stock price will be above, below or the same as the strike price (X) of the option? We'll call this probability P(X).

Sometime in the future, you are going to buy the stock, either in the market at the prevailing price, or at the strike price by exercising your right to buy. From what we learned about discounting, we know that you can put your money on deposit until you take action. The amount of money you need depends upon whether you buy the stock at the prevailing market price (S) or the strike price (X). Let's call these values S and PV(X).

The likely cost of each scenario could be summarised as follows:

Situation 1 = S × P(S)
Situation 2 = PV(X) × P(X)

If the stock price suddenly leapt up then S would increase, as would the probability that the stock could be this price or higher when you wanted to buy it. The value of a call option would increase in these circumstances.

The value of a call option would simply be the difference in value between the two possible worlds:

$$\text{Call option premium} = S \times P(S) - PV(X) \times P(X)$$

Equation 9

As the stock price increased so would the call option price. In effect, we would have something like the 'hockey stick' graph seen in the previous chapter.

You could go through the same process for a put option but, this time, you own the stock and you are definitely going to sell, either at the prevailing market price or at the strike price. The probabilities are now defined as at or below today's price, and the discounting process is seen from the view point of the purchaser (how much money do they need on deposit to buy the stock at either the market price or the strike price), but the logic is the same. What is the difference between the two possible worlds?

$$\text{Put option premium} = PV(X) \times P(X) - S \times P(S)$$

Equation 10

Notice that the positions of the strike price and stock price have reversed compared to the call option example. This is because, as the stock price falls, we are more likely to sell the stock at the strike price.

These two equations are, in essence, the BSM equation for pricing options. It is just probabilities and present values but it was a massive intellectual leap and allowed, for the first time, accurate pricing of options using observable variables everybody could agree upon. It's not putting it too strongly to say Black, Scholes and Merton changed the world forever.

5.2 DAMNED LIES

So far I have simplified some of the concepts of option pricing. In this section we will have a more detailed look at the probability bit, which requires us to dip our toes into the world of statistics.

If you measured the size of the movements of a stock price, and the number of times they occurred, you would get a hump-shaped curve (see figure 17). The distribution would be symmetrical either side of the peak. The mean (the average), the mode (value occurring most often) and median (the middle of the range of possible values) of the movements would be the same and equal to zero. This is called the **normal distribution curve**.

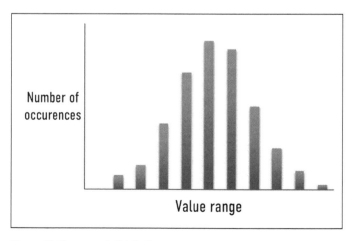

Figure 17: The normal distribution curve

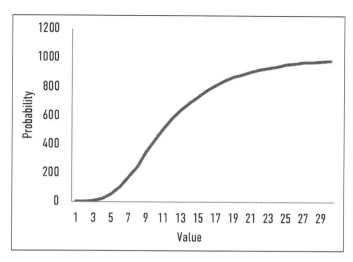

Figure 18: The cumulative normal distribution

Not all of the movements are the same; some are larger and some are smaller than the average movement. The average difference from the average movement is called the **standard deviation**. It can be to the right or left of the peak of the hump, and is a measure of the volatility of a stock or commodity. One standard deviation either side of the mean covers 66% of the possible movements, two standard deviations covers 95%.

If you add up, from the left, the number of occurrences of each possible movement on the normal distribution curve, and plot it against the value, you will create an s-shaped curve. This is called the **cumulative normal distribution** and is, effectively, the area under the normal distribution curve. The corresponding point on the y-axis of the s-shaped curve is equal to the probability of you encountering the value of the x-axis directly below it. As you move from left to right, the probability increases from 0% to 100%. If you count from right to left, you can calculate the probability of encountering a value on the x-axis or above. This process is what is used to calculate the probabilities for use in option pricing; researchers study price movements from market data and derive the probability for use in option pricing models.

There is a complication when discussing stocks. Their *returns* are normally distributed, but their *price movement* distribution is skewed – there are more positive movements. This is because stocks and their dividends should grow with the economy, which means they have a hidden driver built into them, driving the share price upwards over time. But, as the share price increases, to maintain a constant return, the size of each change has to increase, which skews the distribution of the price movements. This skewness is called **log-normal behavior**. Stocks are assumed to exhibit normally distributed *returns* but log-normally distributed share price movements.

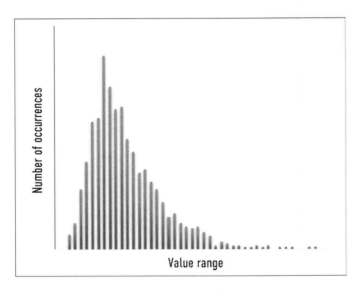

Figure 19: The skewed shape of log-normal distribution

The mathematics of pricing options for stocks takes this skewness into account.

5.3 PRICING A CALL OPTION – THE PROPER WAY

The amount of cash you need to buy a stock some time from now $(T - t)$ is the present value of the stock, if you bought it at the strike price (X), at expiration which, using the continuous discounting equation, is:

$$PV = Xe^{-r(T-t)}$$

Equation 11

where r is the riskless rate of return and $(T - t)$ is the time to expiration.

We are putting our money on deposit in the bank and letting it grow to expiration, assuming we are going to buy the stock at the strike price.

If we substitute our new terms into our simplified equation, we can find out the value of a call option:

$$\text{Call option premium} = S_0 P(S) - Xe^{-r(T-t)}P(X)$$

Equation 12

Where S_0 is the price of the stock today and $P(S)$ and $P(X)$ are the probabilities as previously explained. But we still haven't worked out a way of describing $P(S)$ and $P(X)$.

The probabilities $P(S)$ and $P(X)$ are equal to the cumulative normal distribution associated with the stock price and the strike price of the option. Or, to put it another way, the probability that the stock price and strike price will at least retain their value at expiration.

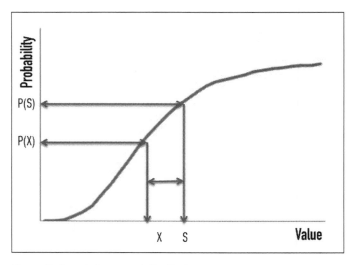

Figure 20: Cumulative normal distribution curve

To get to the final BSM equation, let's call the probability that the stock price will be $S_0\, N(d_1)$, while $N(d_2)$ becomes the probability that the stock price will be the strike price (X). If you placed them onto the cumulative distribution graph, you would get a sense of how an option price moves up and down as the difference between P(X) and P(S) concertinas up and down over time.

So, now, the equation for the value of a call option looks like this:

$$\text{Call option premium} = S_0 N(d_1) - X e^{-r(T-t)} N(d_2)$$

Equation 13

The values of d_1 and d_2 are arrived at using these equations:

$$d_1 = \ln(S_0/X) + (r + \sigma^2/2)(T - t) / \sigma(T - t)^{1/2}$$
$$d_2 = \ln(S_0/X) + (r - \sigma^2/2)(T - t) / \sigma(T - t)^{1/2} = d1 - \sigma(T - t)^{1/2}$$

σ = Volatility of the stock as measured by its standard deviation

r = Risk-free rate

T - t = Time to expiration as a proportion of a year

Another way of writing d_2 is:

$$d2 = d1 - \sigma(T - t)^{1/2}$$

Using d_1 and d_2 we can convert them into the cumulative normal distribution (i.e., probabilities) using standard tables – if you are old-fashioned – or we can use a function in a spreadsheet, as we'll see later. But, by this point, you have everything you need to calculate a non-dividend paying call option on a stock which can only be exercised at expiration. Here's an example:

Thales of Miletus PLC's stock price is $67. Interest rates are currently 5% per annum while the stock has an historic volatility of 10% per annum. What is the value of a 27-day call option with a strike price of $65?

$$\text{Call option premium} = SN(d_1) - Xe^{-r(T-t)}N(d_2)$$
$$Xe^{-r(T-t)} = 65e^{-(0.05 \times 27/365)}$$
$$= 64.76$$

Now:

$$d_1 = \ln(S_0/X) + (r + \sigma^2/2)(T - t) / \sigma(T - t)^{1/2}$$
$$= \ln(67/65) + (0.05 + 0.10^2/2)(27/365) / 0.1 \times (27/365)^{1/2}$$
$$= 0.0303 + 0.0041 / 0.0272$$
$$= 1.2638$$
$$d2 = d_1 - \sigma(T - t)^{1/2}$$
$$= 1.2638 - 0.1 \times (27/365)^{1/2}$$
$$= 1.2638 - 0.0272$$
$$= 1.2366$$

From standard tables of cumulative normal distribution:

$$N(d_1) = 0.8969$$
$$N(d_2) = 0.8919$$
$$\text{Call option premium} = (67 \times 0.8969) - (64.76 \times 0.8919)$$
$$= 60.0893 - 57.7588$$
$$= \$2.33$$

Boom!

5.4   PRICING A PUT OPTION

We can go through exactly the same process to derive the equation for the price of a put option (the right to sell) on a non-dividend paying stock exercised only at expiration (European style).

But since we are looking for when the stock price is *below* a certain value (to the right of the line on the normal distribution), we need the bit not under the curve for our cumulative distribution function so…

$$\text{Put option premium} = Xe^{-r(T-t)} N(-d_2) - S_0 N(-d_1)$$

Equation 14

Note: $N(-d_1)$ and $N(-d_2)$ are the same as $1-N(d_1)$ and $1-N(d_2)$ respectively.

If you were to work it through, using the previous example of Thales of Miletus PLC, you would find that the value of a put option with a $65 strike price (all other conditions exactly the same) would be $0.09 when the stock price is $67.

This is a pretty amazing result because now, with just a few numbers, we can find the value of a European-style non-dividend stock option whether it is a put or a call.

5.5   CALCULATING THE VALUE OF AN OPTION USING EXCEL

So far we have ignored complications like dividends, but it is really quite easy to include these into the BSM equation. First of all, for a stock paying an annual dividend (q), we now have to find the present value of the stock as though it were growing by the dividend yield over the life of the option (the dividend yield becomes your discounting factor). So, our put and call equations become:

$$\text{Value of call option} = S_0 e^{-q(T-t)} N(d_1) - X e^{-r(T-t)} N(d_2)$$

Equation 15

$$\text{Value of a put} = X e^{-r(T-t)} N(-d_2) - S_0 e^{-q(T-t)} N(-d_1)$$

Equation 16

Our equation for d_1 also has an interest rate factor inside of it which can be accounted for by this inclusion of q:

$$d_1 = \ln(S_0/X) + (r - q + \sigma^2/2)(T - t) \,/\, \sigma(T - t)^{1/2}$$

We are now set! There are many elements common to the equations, which we can break down into a number of parts to avoid mistakes:

$$S_0 e^{-q(T-t)}$$
$$X e^{-r(T-t)}$$
$$N(d_1)$$
$$N(d_2)$$
$$\sigma(T - t)^{1/2}$$

To illustrate how this works, let's use our example from before: Thales of Miletus PLC's stock price is $67, interest rates are currently 5% per annum, and the stock has an historic volatility of 10% per annum. What is the value of a 27-day call option with a strike price of $65?

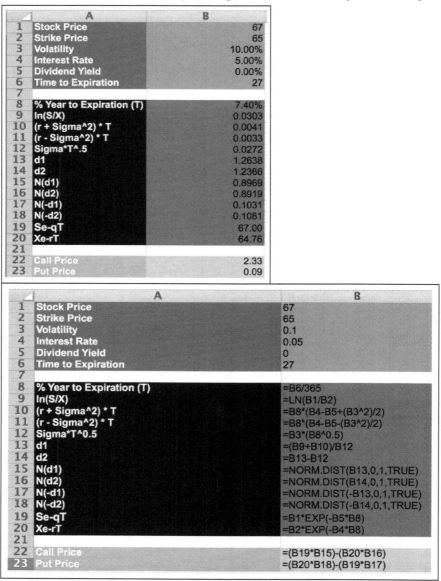

Figure 21: Calculating the price of a call and put option using the same information

The unfamiliar parts of the formulae are the terms $N(d_1)$, $N(d_2)$, $N(-d_2)$, and $N(-d_1)$ – the standard normal cumulative distribution functions.

In Excel, you can easily calculate the standard normal cumulative distribution functions using the NORM.DIST function, which has four parameters:

NORM.DIST(x, mean, standard deviation, cumulative)

x = Link to the cell where you have calculated d1 or d2.

mean = Enter 0, because it is standard normal distribution.

standard deviation = Enter 1, because it is standard normal distribution.

cumulative = Enter TRUE, because it is cumulative.

Don't forget $N(-d_1)$ is the same as $1 - N(d_1)$ if you don't want to go through the effort of programming each $N(x)$. Once you have all the elements defined, it's easy to arrange them to calculate the values of the call and put options (cells B22 and B23).

5.6 STUFF GOES UP AND DOWN – GET USED TO IT

Another important factor needed to value an option is **volatility**. The BSM model won't tell you what it is – you have to estimate it. This isn't so difficult in itself; all you need is some data and well-established statistical equations for the standard deviation and mean, and you are pretty much there. For instance, we can use daily, weekly or monthly stock price data you can easily get from internet resources like Yahoo! Finance.

Technically, we should use continuous compounding to estimate the volatility of a stock:[19]

---

19 See *Options, Futures and Other Derivatives*, John Hull, p.88, for a derivation of these equations.

$$\text{Standard deviation} = \sqrt{\frac{1}{n-1}\Sigma_{i=1}^{n}(u_i - \overline{u})^2}$$

n = Number of observations

S_i = Stock price

ui = $\ln(S_i/S_{i-1})$

$\overline{u}$ = Mean of u_i = $\Sigma_{i=1}^{n} ui/_1$

The annualising factor is the square root of the number of trading days per annum (250). An example may help. Below I've used real stock market data (closing prices) to calculate the volatility of a stock to be 14.3% when considering continuous compounding.[20]

	A	B	C	D	E	F
1	Date	Day Count	Close	Price Change	ui	(ui - Average ui)^2
2	31/01/18	22	235	1.0086	0.0085	0.0001
3	30/01/18	21	233	0.9856	-0.0145	0.0002
4	29/01/18	20	236.4	0.9834	-0.0168	0.0003
5	25/01/18	19	240.4	1.0063	0.0063	0.0000
6	24/01/18	18	238.9	1.0076	0.0076	0.0000
7	23/01/18	17	237.1	1.0025	0.0025	0.0000
8	22/01/18	16	236.5	0.9958	-0.0042	0.0000
9	19/01/18	15	237.5	1.0076	0.0076	0.0000
10	18/01/18	14	235.7	1.0038	0.0038	0.0000
11	17/01/18	13	234.8	1.0047	0.0047	0.0000
12	16/01/18	12	233.7	1.0170	0.0168	0.0003
13	15/01/18	11	229.8	1.0044	0.0044	0.0000
14	12/01/18	10	228.8	1.0155	0.0154	0.0002
15	11/01/18	9	225.3	0.9969	-0.0031	0.0000
16	10/01/18	8	226	0.9947	-0.0053	0.0000
17	09/01/18	7	227.2	1.0089	0.0088	0.0001
18	08/01/18	6	225.2	0.9987	-0.0013	0.0000
19	05/01/18	5	225.5	1.0004	0.0004	0.0000
20	04/01/18	4	225.4	0.9956	-0.0044	0.0000
21	03/01/18	3	226.4	0.9895	-0.0105	0.0001
22	02/01/18	2	228.8	0.9875	-0.0126	0.0002
23	01/01/18	1	231.7	1.0000	0.0000	0.0000
24	29/12/17	-	231.7			
25				Mean	0.0006	0.0017
26						
27					SD	14.30%

Figure 22: Volatility calculation for a real stock

---

20   *Options, Futures and Other Derivatives*, John Hull, p.89.

	A	B	C	D	E	F
1	Date	Day Count	Close	Price Change	ui	(ui - Average ui)^2
2	43131	22	235	=C2/C3	=LN(D2)	=(E2-E$25)^2
3	43130	21	233	=C3/C4	=LN(D3)	=(E3-E$25)^2
4	43129	20	236.4	=C4/C5	=LN(D4)	=(E4-E$25)^2
5	43125	19	240.4	=C5/C6	=LN(D5)	=(E5-E$25)^2
6	43124	18	238.9	=C6/C7	=LN(D6)	=(E6-E$25)^2
7	43123	17	237.1	=C7/C8	=LN(D7)	=(E7-E$25)^2
8	43122	16	236.5	=C8/C9	=LN(D8)	=(E8-E$25)^2
9	43119	15	237.5	=C9/C10	=LN(D9)	=(E9-E$25)^2
10	43118	14	235.7	=C10/C11	=LN(D10)	=(E10-E$25)^2
11	43117	13	234.8	=C11/C12	=LN(D11)	=(E11-E$25)^2
12	43116	12	233.7	=C12/C13	=LN(D12)	=(E12-E$25)^2
13	43115	11	229.8	=C13/C14	=LN(D13)	=(E13-E$25)^2
14	43112	10	228.8	=C14/C15	=LN(D14)	=(E14-E$25)^2
15	43111	9	225.3	=C15/C16	=LN(D15)	=(E15-E$25)^2
16	43110	8	226	=C16/C17	=LN(D16)	=(E16-E$25)^2
17	43109	7	227.2	=C17/C18	=LN(D17)	=(E17-E$25)^2
18	43108	6	225.2	=C18/C19	=LN(D18)	=(E18-E$25)^2
19	43105	5	225.5	=C19/C20	=LN(D19)	=(E19-E$25)^2
20	43104	4	225.4	=C20/C21	=LN(D20)	=(E20-E$25)^2
21	43103	3	226.4	=C21/C22	=LN(D21)	=(E21-E$25)^2
22	43102	2	228.8	=C22/C23	=LN(D22)	=(E22-E$25)^2
23	43101	1	231.7	=C23/C24	=LN(D23)	=(E23-E$25)^2
24	43098	0	231.7			
25				Mean	=AVERAGE(E2:E23)	=SUM(F2:F24)
26						
27					SD	=SQRT(F25/21)*SQRT(250)

Figure 23: Formulae for volatility calculation

But how much data should we use? One month, three months, six months? Should we give more weight to the data closer to the present and less weight to data far in the past? How about a *moving window* of data – a fixed number of data points which incorporates new data while old data drops out of the range? The methods and perspectives on calculating volatility are as varied as the human imagination but the method you choose is crucial, as it will have an enormous effect on your options strategy. Profit-making positions can be turned into loss-making ones costing millions of dollars simply by changing the volatility calculation method. Believe me; I've seen it happen!

The other way of approaching volatility, is to turn the BSM Model on its head and ask what volatility is needed to match the observed market price with the theoretical price? You can keep plugging numbers into our options spreadsheet and gradually zoom in on the market price, or you can use EXCEL functions like 'Goal Seek' which will do the work for you. Goal Seek allows one variable in a calculation to be changed until a desired output is achieved. You could, for instance, ask

Goal Seek to change the volatility number until the calculated option price was equal to the observed market price. This would tell you the implied volatility of the option. Either way, investors end up making a market comparison about, not the value of the option, but whether the volatility is too high (expensive) or too low (cheap) when making their decision to buy or sell options.

5.7   IT'S ALL GREEK TO ME

Including time, volatility, interest rates and dividends into the price of an option changes the profile of an option pay-off diagram considerably; it isn't actually a straight line hockey stick anymore – it's a curve.

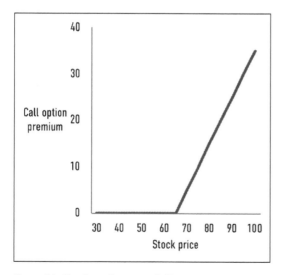

Figure 24: Simple option pay-off diagram

The hockey stick...

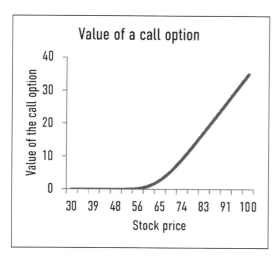

Figure 25: Pay-off with all factors considered

… becomes a curve.

The creation of our pleasing curve might seem like a purely aesthetic nicety but it has real practical consequences. If the price of the option isn't moving in a simple and consistent way, maintaining a perfect hedge will be impossible; there would need to be a lot of tweaking.

For instance, the relationship between the price of the underlying commodity and the movement of an option is called the **delta**. A delta of 0.5 means the option moves by 0.5 for every 1 point movement in the underlying. To recreate the price movement of the stock would require twice as many options as stock. This is known as the **hedge ratio**:

Hedge ratio = 1 / Option delta

Equation 17

So if the delta of the option was 0.5:

Hedge ratio = 1/0.5 = 2

That is, an investor would need twice as many options to replicate the movement of the stock price.

Imagine your option moves up in price, and the delta of the call option increases from 0.5 to 0.75. In order to replicate the price movement of the underlying asset, you would have to reduce your option position from a hedge ratio of x2 to a hedge ratio of x1.333(1/0.75). This is called remaining **delta neutral**. In this case, you would have to sell some of your options, banking profits as you go.

Conversely, if the price of the underlying fell, and the delta of your option fell from 0.5 to 0.25, then you would have to buy more options to maintain the replicating properties of the option position. Not only are you now putting more money into the trade but your total (dealing) cost associated with the position is rising.

This leads to a very important conclusion about the difference between futures and options. **Futures are passive in the sense that you buy or sell a contract and leave the position alone, but options positions have to be managed because the delta of the option is constantly changing**. This is due to the curvature of the option/price pay-off profile – it's an important phenomenon.

To complicate things further, the delta of an option doesn't change in a nice linear fashion. The rate of change of the delta as the price moves is called **gamma** (g). If you have a high gamma option then the delta of the option will move quickly, which means that to remain delta neutral you will have to rebalance your portfolio more often.

If we go back to the BSM option equations, we will find that there are some fixed components and a lot of components which vary over time. What's more important is that each of these variable inputs has an effect on the price of an option; they each have a *price sensitivity*. These price-altering variables are given a Greek symbol (summarised in the table below). Collectively, they are referred to as an option's **Greeks**.

Variable	Greek symbol	Pronounced	Significance
Risk-free rate	ρ	Row (as in 'Row, row, row your boat' but spelled Rho)	Price sensitivity of the option price to changing interest rates by 1%, measured in fractions of the underlying. Not a very significant factor since the financial crisis because interest rates have been low and stable.
Time	Θ	Theta	Price sensitivity of the option price to time, measured in fractions of the underlying. By convention theta is negative as price decay occurs as time passes.
Stock price	Δ	Delta	Sensitivity of an option price to a one-unit price change in the underlying price, measured in fractions one unit.
Volatility	ν	Vega	Sensitivity of an option price to a 1% change in volatility, measured in fractions of one unit.
Change of delta	γ	Gamma	Sensitivity of the delta of an option to a one-unit price change in the underlying, measured in fractions of one unit.

Figure 26: The Greeks of options

There is a full suite of equations to calculate each one of the Greeks. Although they look daunting at first glance, with careful spreadsheet programming all the information needed to calculate them can be found in the description and the examples already given. The one most investors are interested in is the delta of an option because of its role in hedging. To calculate the delta of an option all you need is q, t, $N(d_1)$ and $N(d_2)$:

Call delta = $e_{-qt} \times N(d_1)$

Equation 18

Put delta = $e_{-qt} \times (N(d_1) - 1)$

Equation 19

Just for completeness, here is how you could enhance your options price calculator to determine the delta of a put and call option.

	A	B
1	Stock Price	67
2	Strike Price	65
3	Volatility	12.00%
4	Interest Rate	5.00%
5	Dividend Yield	4.00%
6	Time to Expiration	16
7		
8	% Year to Expiration (T)	4.38%
9	ln(S/X)	0.0303
10	(r + Sigma^2) * T	0.0008
11	(r - Sigma^2) * T	0.0001
12	Sigma*T^0.5	0.0251
13	d1	1.2362
14	d2	1.2111
15	N(d1)	0.8918
16	N(d2)	0.8871
17	N(-d1)	0.1082
18	N(-d2)	0.1129
19	Se-qT	66.88
20	Xe-rT	64.86
21		
22	Call Price	2.11
23	Put Price	0.09
24	Call Delta	0.8902
25	Put Delta	0.1080

Figure 27: Calculation of the delta of a put and call option

	A	B
1	Stock Price	67
2	Strike Price	65
3	Volatility	0.12
4	Interest Rate	0.05
5	Dividend Yield	0.04
6	Time to Expiration	16
7		
8	% Year to Expiration (T)	=B6/365
9	ln(S/X)	=LN(B1/B2)
10	(r + Sigma^2) * T	=B8*(B4-B5+(B3^2)/2)
11	(r - Sigma^2) * T	=B8*(B4-B5-(B3^2)/2)
12	Sigma*T^0.5	=B3*(B8^0.5)
13	d1	=(B9+B10)/B12
14	d2	=B13-B12
15	N(d1)	=NORM.DIST(B13,0,1,TRUE)
16	N(d2)	=NORM.DIST(B14,0,1,TRUE)
17	N(-d1)	=NORM.DIST(-B13,0,1,TRUE)
18	N(-d2)	=NORM.DIST(-B14,0,1,TRUE)
19	Se-qT	=B1*EXP(-B5*B8)
20	Xe-rT	=B2*EXP(-B4*B8)
21		
22	Call Price	=(B19*B15)-(B20*B16)
23	Put Price	=(B20*B18)-(B19*B17)
24	Call Delta	=B15*EXP(-B5*B8)
25	Put Delta	=B17*EXP(-B5*B8)

Figure 28: Formulae behind the calculation of delta

5.8 CONCLUSION

As a teenager, I played rugby on the same team as someone who would later play internationally and become one of the best fullbacks the world has ever seen. As a small boy was carried near-lifeless from the field of play, the soon-to-be national hero had the opportunity to display all the motivational skills that would later elevate him to the captaincy of his national team. He barked at me, "You're terrible – but you're all we've got. Get on!" Critics of the BSM options pricing model take pretty much the same approach. It's not actually very real-world – has lots of assumptions inside of it – but it's all we've got until something better comes along.

Miraculous though the BSM equations are, they only really hold true for the very second you implement them. Immediately afterwards, you will have to keep rebalancing your position to keep the whole thing perfectly hedged as the market moves up and down. The infinitesimal number of times when the BSM model works aren't really very useful in the real world. If frequent rebalancing is inevitable, you really should take transaction costs into account in your overall profit and loss. This also goes for taxes which are not mentioned anywhere in the equations.

You'll notice also that we have steered clear of bond options here – for good reason. They are a subject of their own, mainly because there are additional factors which make the picture more complicated. For instance, as a bond trundles towards its final redemption price, volatility actually declines towards zero. In other words, the volatility is a function of time which is not something the BSM model takes into account. Also, there are those pesky periodic income payments which may be paid during the lifetime of the option. Most serious of all is the internal contradiction of the discounting factors – they are assumed to be constant and yet the idea of an option is to try and model the fact that they vary over time.

Despite all of these drawbacks and criticisms, the BSM model does actually provide options prices remarkably close to those observed in the market. Whether this is because everybody uses the model and so option prices are driven to those levels or because, despite its approximations and idealisations, it does offer some kind of universal truth, we may never know. But until someone comes up with something better – it's the best we have.

Now get yer boots – yer on!

6. USING FUTURES IN A PORTFOLIO: IF I HAVE A FUTURE, I HAVE A FUTURE

U sing derivatives to manage risk, or to speculate, is a huge business. Even today – a decade after the financial crisis of 2008, which was largely attributed to the unintentional concentration of risks in the banking system due to derivatives – there are still enormous derivatives positions floating around the financial system. In 2011, three years after the crash, it was estimated that the top five US banks alone still had derivatives exposure of over $40trn. On closer examination, some of the most prestigious names in banking look like a gigantic bet on the markets; they can have derivatives positions with a notional value of between 25 and 55 times their assets.[21]

The image of derivatives isn't helped by a roll call of history's greatest financial losses. It is peppered with institutions and individuals who have, either intentionally or unintentionally, been caught up in market movements which turned profit-making strategies into loss-making headlines in the blink of an eye. Take a look at this list of known offenders:

21 www.zerohedge.com/news/2014-09-25/5-us-banks-each-have-more-40-trillion-dollars-exposure-derivatives

Position	Nominal amount	Country	Company	Sources of loss	Year	Person associated with incident
1	USD 9.0bn	United Kingdom	JP Morgan Chase	Credit default swaps	2012	Bruno Iksil
2	USD 8.7bn	United States	Morgan Stanley	Credit default swaps	2008	Howie Hubler
3	USD 7.0bn	France	Société Générale	European index futures	2008	Jerome Kerviel
4	USD 6.7bn	United States	Amaranth Advisors	Gas futures	2006	Brian Hunter
5	USD 5.9bn	United States	Long Term Capital Management	Interest rate and equity derivatives	1998	John Meriwether
6	USD 3.5bn	Japan	Sumitomo Corporation	Copper futures	1996	Yasuo Hamanaka
7	USD 2.4bn	Brazil	Aracruz	Foreign exchange options	2008	Isac Zagury and Rafael Sotero
8	USD 2.4bn	United States	Orange County	Leveraged bond investments	1994	Robert Citron
9	USD 2.3bn	Germany	Metallgesellschaft	Oil futures	1993	Heinz Schimmmelbusch
10	USD 2.1bn	Japan	Showa Shell Sekiyu	Foreign exchange forwards	1993	Treasury staff unauthorised dealing

Figure 29: History's greatest known derivatives losses

What this table tells you is that making mistakes in the derivatives markets is truly a global enterprise. No single nation has the monopoly on greed, stupidity or just bad luck, although some appear to crop up with greater regularity than others.

The financial health warning accompanying the dark side of derivatives is only there for the extreme cases; the rare circumstances when use turns to abuse, and intentional uses have unintended consequences. There are a lot of everyday uses of derivatives that simply don't fall into this category. What follows here are some everyday examples of the use of futures that every fund manager could take advantage of.

6.1 MAKING A REAL ASSET OF YOURSELF

Let's start off with the best-kept secret in the financial markets. It's a tiny equation and it looks like this:

Market = Cash + Future

Equation 20

This equation says you can replicate the movement of the market if you buy a future and hold cash. Let's work through an example.

If you had, say, $100,000 in the bank and wanted to put the equivalent into the stock market, you could buy futures contracts to the notional value of $100,000. Your portfolio would track the market pretty much exactly. You don't have to own individual stocks; there are no dividends to collect; there are no brokers analysts involved; and it's all done with a single transaction. It's a piece of magic.

There are a couple of important rearrangements of this wondrous piece of work. The most important of which is:

Cash = Market - Future

Equation 21

In other words, you could make your $100,000 market portfolio *look like cash in the bank* by selling futures (go short) to the notional value of $100,000. The total portfolio would stop going up and down in value with the swings of the market because any profit or losses made on the long position in stocks would be balanced by the short position in futures.

This could be very useful if, for instance, you expected the market to fall but didn't want to go through the costly and time-consuming process of selling your portfolio of stocks. Of course, the converse is also true – if the market rose then the portfolio wouldn't move in value which would be an opportunity lost. If your investment performance is being measured against the returns of the market, you would underperform.

If you can invest money when you expect the market to rise, and you can protect your portfolio when you expect it to fall, just by using the futures market, you may be tempted to start thinking that you could, maybe, try and catch some of those mini-waves surging through the markets week-by-week, day-by-day or hour-by-hour. If you are starting to think like this – congratulations, you just caught the trading bug and a lifetime of sleepless nights.

But leaving the prospect of day trading aside for a moment, in the following sections we are going to look at the process of investing money in the stock, bond and currency markets using derivatives. Then we are going to combine all three markets together to show how you can change the structure of an entire portfolio using futures.

6.2 INVESTING MONEY IN THE EQUITY MARKET USING FUTURES

In the following examples we are going to repeat a four-step process. No matter whether we are talking about equities, bonds or currencies, it looks like this:

Step 1 – Calculate how much money you have to invest

Step 2 – Work out how much each futures contract is worth

Step 3 – Divide Step 1/Step 2 to calculate the approximate number of contracts needed

Step 4 – Round to the nearest whole number of contracts (you can't buy fractions of a futures contract)

6.3 EXAMPLE OF INVESTING MONEY USING STOCK INDEX FUTURES

Let's imagine you have a $100m portfolio and you wish to invest $15m in the US stock market (S&P 500 index) which is currently trading at 2,550. A futures contract on the S&P 500 has a standard contract size of $250 per index point.[22]

Now we can begin our calculation:

Step 1 – Calculate how much money you have to invest = $15,000,000

Step 2 – Calculate how much each contract is worth = $250 × Index = $250 × 2,550 = $637,500

Step 3 – Divide Step 1/Step 2 to find the number of contracts needed = 15,000,000/637,500 = 23.52

Step 4 – Round to the nearest whole number of contracts = 24

You'll notice when purchasing 24 contracts that you will have marginally overinvested your target of $15m. You could round down to 23 contracts, but this will entail a marginal underinvestment. This lack of precision is one of the downsides of exchange traded futures.

---

22   To save time, at the end of this chapter there is a list of the major equity index futures along with their Bloomberg name (ticker). Notice that the Bloomberg ticker isn't on the <Comdty> key where you usually find derivatives. For some reason, they are on the <Index> key.

	A	B	C			B	C
1	Step 1	Fund Size	100,000,000		1	Fund Size	100000000
2		Cash	15,000,000		2	Cash	15000000
3					3		
4		Index Level (S&P 500)	2,550.00		4	Index Level (S&P 500)	2550
5	Step 2	Value of 1Pt	250		5	Value of 1Pt	250
6		Contract Value	637,500		6	Contract Value	=C5*C4
7					7		
8	Step 3	Number of Contracts	23.53		8	Number of Contracts	=C2/C6
9	Step 4	Number of Contracts (Rounded)	24		9	Number of Contracts (Rounded)	=ROUND(C8,0)
10					10		
11					11		
12					12		

Figure 30: Calculating the required number of futures contracts

There is nothing more to it. You'll need money for the initial and variation margin as the market moves around, but you have gained exposure to the market for your portfolio much quicker than trying to replicate the entire S&P index by purchasing all 500 stocks in precisely the right weightings. I have missed out brokerage fees because they are trivial – a couple of US dollars per contract, for instance, which is less than 0.02% of your investment. Compare this with the cost of trading an entire portfolio of equities, and you should start to understand the overwhelming advantage of using derivatives to gain quick, cheap exposure to the markets. There really isn't a contest – derivatives win every time.

6.4 BONDS VERSUS EQUITIES IS REALLY NORTH VERSUS SOUTH

Bond managers should come from the north of England. There is something about the dour realism of the north that seems to suit bond management. By contrast, equity managers should come from the south of England. You need a sunny, optimistic disposition to be a successful equity manager; it's a world of possibilities.

The major concern of your average bond manager is the sensitivity of their bond portfolio to bond yields moving up and down with the economic and market cycles.[23] As a group, they genuinely benefit from, and look forward to, economic disasters. These cause interest rates and bond yields to decline, which is good for what they do for a living. Here's why.

Without going into too much detail, a couple of rules apply to bonds:

- as yields rise, prices fall

- as yields fall, prices rise

- the longer the maturity of a bond (the time until you get your money back), the more the price moves as yields rise and fall

- the price sensitivity of a bond, as yields change, is called **duration**.

This confusing set of relationships looks like this for those of you with a mathematical bent:

$$\Delta P = -\Delta Y \times \text{Duration}$$

Equation 22

where ΔP is the price change and ΔY is the bond yield change.

It's pretty useful to know this. Take for example a 10-year maturity bond with a duration of seven. What is the price change if the yield falls by 0.5%?

Using our equation, it's easy to calculate this:

$$\Delta P = -(-0.5) \times 7$$
$$\Delta P = 0.5 \times 7$$
$$\Delta P = 3.5$$

---

23   At this point can I recommend that you purchase a copy of *Bonds in a Day* by Stewart Cowley.

So if yields fall by 0.5%, the price of the bond rises by 3.5 points. Similarly, if yields rise by 0.5%, the price of the bond would fall by 3.5 points. This is why people obsess about the rise and fall of bond yields and predicting the economic cycle which controls them.

Fortunately, as in the case of equities, government bond futures contracts exist which allow investors to access the bond markets without actually building a portfolio of bonds. Each contract trades on an exchange and is representative of either a collection of bonds, or some kind of notional bond, which defines the characteristics of the bond future. If you have access to Bloomberg, type WBF <GO> and you will see the screen below which shows you a range of government bond futures. Select one of them, type DES and you will get the details of the contract.

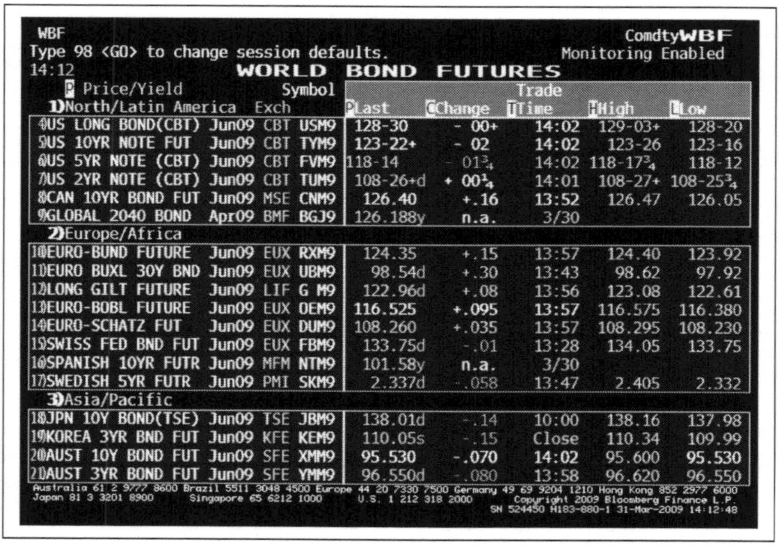

Figure 31: Bond futures as seen on Bloomberg

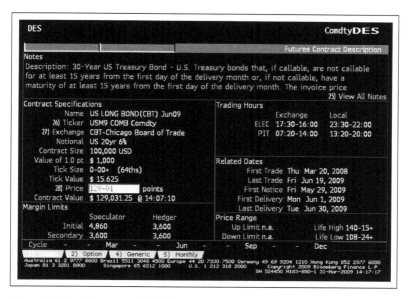

Figure 32: The DES screen of the US Long Bond Future

Stock index futures allow you to deliver the constituents of the index on the expiry date. It's the same for bond futures contracts. At any time, there are a limited number of qualifying bonds suitable for delivery at expiration of a futures contract. The choice of which one should be delivered comes down to how much money it will cost to get hold of each bond. Obviously, the most popular qualifying bond will be the one costing the least to get hold of, and is known as the **cheapest-to-deliver** (CTD).[24]

We need a way of relating the value of the CTD to the price of the bond future. This is called the **conversion factor**. So:

CTD = Future × Conversion factor

---

24   See table below for the most popular futures contracts specifications and how the cheapest-to-deliver is worked out.

Equation 23

or putting it another way:

Future = CTD/Conversion factor

Equation 24

Every bond deliverable has its own unique conversion factor. We can use this to relate duration of the CTD to the apparent price movement of the future through the following equation:

Duration of future = Duration of CTD/Conversion factor

Equation 25

This is very useful to know because now we can start using futures, instead of buying and selling bonds, to manage the price volatility of a portfolio.

6.5 EXAMPLE OF INVESTING MONEY USING GOVERNMENT BOND FUTURES

So let's use a futures contract to cope with two of the most common situations in bond portfolios: to cover a cash in-flow and to adjust the duration of an existing portfolio.

Imagine you have a bond portfolio of $100m and a client gives you an extra $15m. You need the portfolio to be fully exposed to the bond market at all times so you have to invest.

Let's buy bond futures with the same value as the $15m you have been given. For the purposes of this exercise we know the following things:

1. The value of each contract is $100,000.

2. The futures price is $106.

3. The duration of the cheapest to deliver is 10.3.

4. The conversion factor is 1.1484.

Let's remind ourselves of the four-step process:

Step 1 – Calculate how much money you have to invest

Step 2 – Calculate how much each futures contract is worth

Step 3 – Divide Step 1/Step 2 to get the approximate number of contracts needed

Step 4 – Round to the nearest whole number of contracts (you can't buy fractions of a contract)

We can summarise this in the spreadsheet below. It's an incredibly powerful piece of work.

	A	B	C
1	Step	Factor	Amount
2	Step 1	Fund Size	100,000,000
3		Cash to Invest	15,000,000
4		Fund Duration	4.55
5		CTD Duration	10.3
6		Conversion Factor	1.1484
7			
8		Futures Price	129
9	Step 2	Value of a Contract	100,000
10		Contract Value	129,000
11		Duration of Future	9.0
12			
13	Step 3	Number of Contracts	116.3
14	Step 4	Number of Contracts (Rounded)	116.0
15		New Duration	5.1
16		Duration Change	0.6
17			

	A	B	C
1	Step	Factor	Amount
2	Step 1	Fund Size	100000000
3		Cash to Invest	15000000
4		Fund Duration	4.55
5		CTD Duration	10.3
6		Conversion Factor	1.1484
7			
8		Futures Price	129
9	Step 2	Value of a Contract	100000
10		Contract Value	=C9*C8/100
11		Duration of Future	=C5/C6
12			
13	Step 3	Number of Contracts	=C3/C10
14	Step 4	Number of Contracts (Rounded)	=ROUND(C13,0)
15		New Duration	=(((C14*C10)*C11)+(C2*C4))/(C2+C3)
16		Duration Change	=C15-C4
17			

Figure 33: Four-step process for calculating an investment in bonds using futures

As an added extra bonus, we can work out the change of duration of the fund (cell C16) by multiplying the duration of the futures contract by the proportion of the new fund invested. As you can see, the fund duration has increased from 4.5 to 5.1 after purchasing the futures contracts, i.e., it has become more sensitive to the movement of yields in the bond market.

Bond managers like to set the duration of a fund to a specific target. You can do this using a futures contract as the following example will show. Your client has a portfolio of $100m containing $15m in cash. The total fund has a 4.5 duration. You want to set the duration of the fund to 5.5 using the futures market. The details of the bond contract are as before. How many contracts do you buy?

You can treat the futures as just another addition to the portfolio (like you would any bond). So the contribution to the overall duration will be:

Duration of futures = F% × Duration of CTD

To add one unit of duration (5.5 - 4.5), you need to work out the percentage of the portfolio that should be invested in the futures market (F%).

F% = Duration of futures/Duration of CTD

In this case:

F% = 1/9 = 11% in round numbers

As the total size of the portfolio is \$115m, it's pretty straightforward to work out how many contracts you would need to invest 11% of the portfolio.

	A	B	C
1	Step 1	Invested Amount	100,000,000
2		Available Cash	15,000,000
3		Total Fund	115,000,000
4		Fund Total Duration	4.5
5		Target Duration	5.5
6		CTD Duration	10.3
7		Conversion Factor	1.1484
8			
9		Futures Price	129
10	Step 2	Value of a Contract	100,000
11		Contract Value	129,000
12		Duration of Future	9.0
13			
14			
15	Step 3	Duration Change Required	1.0
16		Pct Fund to Invest in the Future	11%
17		Value to Invest in Future	12,821,942
18		Number of Contracts	99.4
19	Step 4	Number of Contracts (Rounded)	99
20			
21		Cash Used	12,821,942
22		New Cash Available	2,178,058

	A	B	C
1	Step 1	Invested Amount	100000000
2		Available Cash	15000000
3		Total Fund	=C1+C2
4		Fund Total Duration	4.5
5		Target Duration	5.5
6		CTD Duration	10.3
7		Conversion Factor	1.1484
8			
9		Futures Price	129
10	Step 2	Value of a Contract	100000
11		Contract Value	=C10*C9/100
12		Duration of Future	=C6/C7
13			
14			
15	Step 3	Duration Change Required	=C5-C4
16		Pct Fund to Invest in the Future	=C15/C12
17		Value to Invest in Future	=C16*C3
18		Number of Contracts	=C17/C11
19	Step 4	Number of Contracts (Rounded)	=ROUND(C18,0)
20			
21		Cash Used	=C17
22		New Cash Available	=C2-C21

Figure 34: Process for calculating how to control portfolio duration using futures

So you need to buy 99 contracts to meet the target duration of the fund. In this example, there is a check on the amount of notional cash used or **covered** by the futures contract. The cash used (cell C21) is only $12,821,942 which is less than the available $15m, which is good.

Now change the target duration in the spreadsheet to 6.5 and look at the cash used (see figure below). Clearly, investing over $25m would exceed the available cash of $15m and send the fund notionally overdrawn. Except it wouldn't. In reality, you only put a fraction of the total cost down when you buy a future (the **initial margin**), so all you would be doing is creating a *liability* of about $7.3m which you could get rid of at any time by closing out the position before expiration. In the meantime, the fund would be leveraged (over invested) by 6%, which means you will make excess returns if yields fall (prices rise), but lose more than expected if yields rise (prices fall).

	A	B	C
4		**Fund Total Duration**	4.5
5		**Target Duration**	6.5
6		**CTD Duration**	10.3
7		**Conversion Factor**	1.1484
8			
9		**Futures Price**	129
10	Step 2	**Value of a Contract**	100,000
11		**Contract Value**	129,000
12		**Duration of Future**	9.0
13			
14			
15	Step 3	**Duration Change Required**	2.0
16		**Pct Fund to Invest in the Future**	22%
17		**Value to Invest in Future**	25,643,883
18		**Number of Contracts**	198.8
19	Step 4	**Number of Contracts (Rounded)**	199
20			
21		**Cash Used**	25,643,883
22		**New Cash Available**	(10,643,883)
23			

Figure 35: Increasing bond portfolio duration with leverage using futures

Gearing, or leveraging, money like this isn't confined to the bond markets; you can do it just as easily with equities and anything else for which a futures contract exists. Hedge funds do this on a daily basis and don't restrict themselves to over-investing by a trifling 6% of their portfolio value. Try 300% or 400%. The daily swings in profit and loss of their futures accounts can be extreme, which accounts for the high returns and, on occasion, heavy losses they deliver. This also explains why, from time to time, you see hedge funds go bust – they just guessed wrong and the fund was wiped out in a day or so because of an unforeseen event. When the hedge fund Amaranth went out of business in 2006, it lost $6bn dollars in a week. It was reportedly geared by 800% through speculating on gas futures contracts which went the wrong way.[25]

	A	B	C
1	Step 1	Invested Amount	100,000,000
2		Available Cash	15,000,000
3		Total Fund	115,000,000
4		Fund Total Duration	4.5
5		Target Duration	2.5
6		CTD Duration	10.3
7		Conversion Factor	1.1484
8			
9		Futures Price	129
10	Step 2	Value of a Contract	100,000
11		Contract Value	129,000
12		Duration of Future	9.0
13			
14			
15	Step 3	Duration Change Required -	2.0
16		Pct Fund to Invest in the Future	-22%
17		Value to Invest in Future -	25,643,883
18		Number of Contracts	-198.8
19	Step 4	Number of Contracts (Rounded)	-199
20			
21		Cash Used	(25,643,883)
22		New Cash Available	40,643,883

Figure 36: Reducing a bond portfolio duration using futures

You can use the same spreadsheet to *reduce* the duration of the portfolio. Try reducing the target duration from 4.5 to 2.5. The number of contracts required to achieve this is minus 199. In other words, selling (shorting) 199 bond futures contracts will reduce the duration of the portfolio.

So using bond futures you can easily invest money, increase the duration, reduce the duration or, if it's allowed, leverage the portfolio. It's really fast, really simple and really cheap. All you need to know is a few facts and a conversion factor.

---

25   www.thefirstpost.co.uk/index.php?menuID=2&subID=931&p=2

6.6 MAKING PROFITS FROM FALLING BOND MARKETS

Bond managers have had it easy for a long time. Besides a few uncomfortable moments in the 1970s, global bond yields have fallen (prices have risen) since the time US President Ronald Reagan and UK Prime Minister Margaret Thatcher were making goo-goo eyes at each other in the 1980s. As I write, we sit at an all-time low of bond yields due to a combination of the financial crisis of 2008, historically low interest rates and the artificial suppression of bond yields by global central banks. Things became so extreme during 2016 that investors were paying the Bundesbank for the privilege of owning its bonds; German government debt had negative bond yields.

Only time will tell how this ends but it has to be a fair bet that yields will rise again one day, sending bond prices into a tailspin. As a bond manager, there won't be much you will be able to do about it besides reduce your duration (price volatility), to the lowest point allowed, in order to minimise your losses. But what if you are a greedy little so-and-so and want to make money as bond prices fall – is this possible?

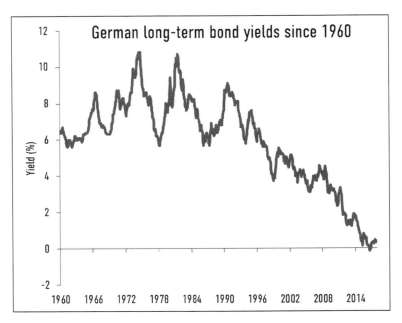

Figure 37: How low can bond yields go? (Data source: Federal Reserve)

When stock markets fall, equity portfolio managers can make money by selling short (i.e., selling something they don't own) in the hope of, one day, buying back at a lower price and pocketing the difference as a profit. Bonds are no different and you can achieve this using government bond futures. In contrast to an ordinary bond portfolio, the duration of a short bond portfolio is *negative* instead of positive.

Using your spreadsheet, change the target duration to -2.5. The same calculation as before instructs you to *sell* 696 futures contracts – creating a negative duration portfolio which can now benefit from *falling* bond prices (rising yields). Cool eh!

	A	B	C
1	Step 1	Invested Amount	100,000,000
2		Available Cash	15,000,000
3		Total Fund	115,000,000
4		Fund Total Duration	4.5
5		Target Duration	-2.5
6		CTD Duration	10.3
7		Conversion Factor	1.1484
8			
9		Futures Price	129
10	Step 2	Value of a Contract	100,000
11		Contract Value	129,000
12		Duration of Future	9.0
13			
14			
15	Step 3	Duration Change Required -	7.0
16		Pct Fund to Invest in the Future	-78%
17		Value to Invest in Future -	89,753,592
18		Number of Contracts	-695.8
19	Step 4	Number of Contracts (Rounded)	-696
20			
21		Cash Used	(89,753,592)
22		New Cash Available	104,753,592

Figure 38: Creating a negative duration using bond futures

This is an important result because now it is possible to create a bond portfolio possessing the unique ability to rise in value when bond yields are rising *or* falling. This is the essence of **total return** or **absolute return** fund management – creating portfolios with the ability to rise in value, or not lose value, in a range of circumstances, not just when your chosen asset class is in favour. There is an entire industry built on this lipsmacking notion.

6.7 CHANGING CURRENCY EXPOSURES USING FUTURES

You may wish to change the foreign exchange exposure of a portfolio using currency futures but, and this is really important, you have to be very careful about the terms of currency futures contracts. For example, the underlying amounts can vary. In practical terms, the mechanism employed to change currency allocations using futures is the same as the one we have been using for stocks and bonds, but the terms of currency futures constructs must be carefully incorporated into your calculations.

Currency futures are quoted in terms of the currency you are buying with an implied sale of another currency. So, for example, the USD/euro futures contract on CME is traded in lots of €125,000 per contract with an implied sale of an amount of US dollars dictated by the futures contract price. At the end of the chapter I've provided details of the main currency futures quoted on CME.

We are going to use the same four-step plan outlined in section 6.5 to work out the number of contracts required to change the currency allocation of a portfolio. From a starting portfolio we are going to try and hit a new allocation of 19% USD, 25% euro, 16% GBP and 40% Japanese yen. For convenience, we'll set the portfolio size as $100m and the base currency of the portfolio as US Dollars. Step 1: we work out the amount needed in USD terms to get to the new allocation and convert into the new currency. Step 2: input the contract size of the relevant future. Step 3: divide the amount by the contract size. Step 4: round to the nearest whole contract.

	A	B	C	D	E	F	G
1		Fund Size	100,000,000				
2			USD	EURO	GBP	JPY	Total
3		Total	42%	16%	9%	33%	100%
4							
5		New Allocation	19%	25%	16%	40%	100%
6		Change	-23%	9%	6%	6%	-2%
7							
8		Value (USD)	-$23,000,000	$9,000,000	$6,000,000	$6,000,000	
9	Step 1	FX Rate	1	0.8	0.56	118	
10		Value (Local)	- 23,000,000	€7,200,000	£3,360,000	¥708,000,000	
11							
12	Step 2	Contract Size		€125,000	£62,500	¥12,500,000	
13							
14	Step 3	Number of Contracts		57.6	53.8	56.6	
15							
16	Step 4	Number of Contracts (Rounded)	0	58	54	57	

	A	B	C	D	E	F	G
1		Fund Size	100000000				
2			USD	EURO	GBP	JPY	Total
3		Total	0.42	0.16	0.09	0.33	=SUM(C3:F3)
4							
5		New Allocation	0.19	0.25	0.16	0.4	=SUM(C5:F5)
6		Change	=C5-C3	=D5-D3	0.06	0.06	=SUM(C6:F6)
7							
8		Value (USD)	=C6*C1	=D6*C1	=E6*C1	=F6*C1	
9	Step 1	FX Rate	1	0.8	0.56	118	
10		Value (Local)	=C8*C9	=D8*D9	=E8*E9	=F8*F9	
11							
12	Step 2	Contract Size		125000	62500	12500000	
13							
14	Step 3	Number of Contracts		=D10/D12	=E10/E12	=F10/F12	
15							
16	Step 4	Number of Contracts (Rounded)	=ROUND(C14,0)	=ROUND(D14,0)	=ROUND(E14,0)	=ROUND(F14,0)	

Figure 39: Changing the currency allocation of a portfolio using futures

This time, to change the currency allocation in the portfolio, trades would be sent through the dealing system to buy 58 USD/EURO contracts, 54 USD/GBP contracts and 57 USD/JPY contracts.

6.8 CONCLUSION

Congratulations – you now have all the tools necessary to be a fully-fledged active fund manager. Using futures to manage a portfolio doesn't help you predict how the markets are going to evolve but they make it much easier to implement whatever strategy you decide to use. And to make your journey into the world of futures even easier, the appendix to this chapter holds a whole host of contract specifications to set you on your way. There's even a page from investing.com where, if you don't own a Bloombery terminal, you can watch a bewildering array of numbers flicker up and down all day.

But don't get carried away with the idea that trading futures and constantly tweaking portfolios is the panacea for investment performance. There are some very influential investors who say the less you trade the better your performance. When asked what his preferred holding period was for a stock, Warren Buffett, the legendary portfolio manager of Berkshire Hathaway Inc., replied "forever".[26] So if you want to design a winning portfolio, you are best off:

- having a vision for the future,

- implementing it in the simplest and cheapest way you can,

- holding on to it for as long as you can without going out of business.

---

26 www.investopedia.com/financial-edge/0210/rules-that-warren-buffett-lives-by.aspx

Contract	Underlying	Notional value	Exchange	Tick size	Tick value	Cycle	Bloomberg ticker
Dow Jones Index Future (US)	Dow Jones Industrial Average Index	$10 × index	Chicago Board of Trade (CBOT)	1	$10	Mar, Jun, Sep, Dec	DJA Index
S&P 500 Future (US)	S&P 500 Index	$250 × index	Chicago Mercantile Exchange (CME)	0.10	$25	Mar, Jun, Sep, Dec	SPA Index
DJ Euro Stoxx 50 (Europe)	Type SX5E Index to see stocks	€10 × index	Eurex (EUX)	1	€10	Mar, Jun, Sep, Dec	VGA Index
FTSE 100 Index Future (UK)	Type UKX Index to see underlying	£10 × index	LIFFE (LIF)	0.5	£5	Mar, Jun, Sep, Dec	Z A Index
CAC40 Future (France)	Type CAC Index to see underlying	€10 × index	Euronext Paris (EOP)	0.5	€5	Calendar months	CFA Index
DAX Index Future (Germany)	Type DAX Index to see underlying	€25 × index	Eurex (EUX)	0.5	€25	Mar, Jun, Sep, Dec	GXA Index
Swiss Market Index Future	Type SMI Index to see underlying	SFr10 × index	Eurex (EUX)	1	SFr10	Mar, Jun, Sep, Dec	SMA Index
NIKKEI 225 (Japan)	Type NKY Index to see underlying	¥1,000 × index	Osaka Securities Exchange (OSE)	10	¥10,000	Mar, Jun, Sep, Dec	NKA Index
Hang Seng Index Future (Hong Kong)	Type HIS Index to see underlying	HK$50 × index	Hong Kong Futures Exchange (HKG)	1	HK$50	Calendar months	HIA Index

Figure 40: Equity index futures

Contract	Nominal	Quoted	Tick size/ value	Options available	Bloomberg ticker
USD/Euro	€125,000	$/€	0.0001/$12.5	Yes	ECA Curncy
USD/Swiss Franc	SFr125,000	Cents/SFr	0.01/$12.5	Yes	SFA Curncy
USD/ Sterling	£62,500	Cents/GBP	0.01/$6.25	Yes	BPA Curncy
Sterling/ Euro	£125,000	GBP/Euro	0.00005/£6.25	Yes	RPA Curncy
JPY/USD	¥12,500,000	Cents/100 yen	0.01/$12.5	Yes	JYA Curncy
CAD/USD	C$100,000	Cents/C$	0.01/$10	Yes	CDA Curncy
AUD/USD	A$100,000	Cents/A$	0.01/$10	Yes	ADA Curncy
NZD/USD	NZ$100,000	Cents/NZ$	0.01/$10	Yes	NVA Curncy

Figure 41: Foreign exchange futures

Contract	Underlying	Qualifying bonds	Notional value	Exchange	Tick size	Tick value	Expiration cycle	Bloomberg ticker
US Long Bond	20-yr yielding 6%	>15 yrs	100,000	Chicago Board of Trade (CBT)	1/64	$15.625	Mar, Jun, Sep, Dec	USA Comdty
US 10-yr Note	10-yr yielding 6%	>6.5 but less than 10 yrs	100,000	Chicago Board of Trade (CBT)	1/64	$15.625	Mar, Jun, Sep, Dec	TYA Comdty
US 5-yr Note	5-yr yielding 6%	4 yrs 2 months – 5 yrs 3 months	100,000	Chicago Board of Trade (CBT)	1/128	$7.8125	Mar, Jun, Sep, Dec	FVA Comdty
US 2-yr Note	2-yr yielding 6%	1 yr 9 months – 2 yrs	200,000	Chicago Board of Trade (CBT)	1/128	$15.625	Mar, Jun, Sep, Dec	TUA Comdty
Euro - BUXL 30-yr	30-yr yielding 4%	24–35 yrs	100,000	EUX (Eurex)	0.02	€20	Mar, Jun, Sep, Dec	UBA Comdty
Euro Bond Future (10-yr)	10-yr yielding 6%	8.5–10.5 yrs	100,000	EUX (Eurex)	0.01	€10	Mar, Jun, Sep, Dec	RXA Comdty
Long Gilt Future	10-yr yielding 6%	8.75–13 yrs	100,000	LIFFE (LIF)	0.01	£10	Mar, Jun, Sep, Dec	G A Comdty
Japan 10-yr Bond (TSE)	10-yr yielding 6%	7–11 yrs	1,000,000	TSE	0.01	¥10,000	Mar, Jun, Sep, Dec	JBA Comdty
Australian 10-yr Bond Futures	10-yr yielding 6%	At least 10 yrs to maturity	100,000	SFE	0.005	A$43.18	Mar, Jun, Sep, Dec	XMA Comdty

Figure 42: Government bond futures

There are numerous places you can get up-to-date contract specifications. For instance, using the Specification tab in the stock index section on Investing.com, a trading platform, gives you all you need to understand the underlying characteristics of many of the available derivatives contracts.

Investing.com   EUR/USD or AAPL

CFD Service | your capital is at risk

Real Time Streaming Futures Quotes (CFDs)

| Price | Performance | Technical | Specification | Candlestick Patterns | | Download Data |

Index :	Symbol :	Exchange :	Contract Size	Months	Point Value
Dow 30	YM	CBOT	$5 x Dow Jones	HMUZ	1 = $5
S&P 500	ES	CME	$50 x Index Price	HMUZ	1 = $50
Nasdaq	NQ	CME	$20 x Nasdaq 100	HMUZ	1 = $20
SmallCap 2000	TF	ICE	$100 x Russell 2000	HMUZ	1 = $100
S&P 500 VIX	VX	CBOE	$1,000 x VIX Index	FGHJKMNQUVXZ	1 = $1000
DAX	FDAX	Eurex	€25 x DAX	HMUZ	1 = €25
CAC 40	FCE	Euronext	€10 x CAC 40	FGHJKMNQUVXZ	1 = €10
FTSE 100	Z	LIFFE	£10 x Index Price	HMUZ	1 = £10
Euro Stoxx 50	FESX	Eurex	€10 x Euro Stoxx 50	HMUZ	1 = €10
FTSE MIB	FIB	Borsa Italiana	€5 x FTSE MIB	HMUZ	1 = €5
SMI	FSMI	Eurex	CHF10 x SMI	HMUZ	1 = CHF10
IBEX 35	IBEX	BME	€10 x IBEX 35	FGHJKMNQUVXZ	1 = €10
ATX	ATX	Eurex	€10 x ATX	HMUZ	1 = €10
WIG20	FW20	WSE	zł10 x WIG20	HMUZ	1 = zł10
AEX	FTI	Euronext	€200 x AEX 25	FGHJKMNQUVXZ	1 = €200
BUX	BUX	BSE	Ft10 x BUX	MZ	1 = Ft100
RTS	RIRTS	MICEX	RUB x RTS	HMUZ	
OBX	OBX	Oslo	NOK100 x OBX	FGHMUXZ	1 = kr100
OMXS30	S30	NASDAQ OMX	SEK100 x OMXS30	HMUZ	1 = kr100
Greece 20	ATF	ATHEX	5 EUR x FTSE/ATHEX Large Cap	FGHJKMNQUVXZ	1 = €5
IBovespa	IND	BM&F Bovespa	R$1 x iBovespa	FGHJKMNQUVXZ	1 = R$1
BMV IPC	IPC	MexDer	Mex$10 x IPC	FGHJKMNQUVXZ	1 = MXN10000
Nikkei 225	NK	OSE	¥1,000 x Nikkei 225	HMUZ	1 = ¥1000
TOPIX	TPX	OSE	¥10000 x TOPIX	HMUZ	1 = ¥10000
Hang Seng	HIS	HKEx	HK$50 x Hang Seng	FGHJKMNQUVXZ	1 = HK$50
China H-Shares	HHI	HKEx	HK$50 x China H-Shares	FGHJKMNQUVXZ	1 = $1
CSI 300			CNY300 x CSI 300	FGHJKMNQUVXZ	1 = CNY300
China A50	SFC	SGX	$1 x China A50	HMUZ	1 = $1
S&P/ASX 200	AP	ASX	A$25 x S&P/ASX 200	HMUZ	1 = A$25
Singapore MSCI	SG	SIMEX	S$100 x SGX MSCI Singapore	FGHJKMNQUVXZ	1 = S$100
Nifty 50	IN	SIMEX	$2 x Nifty 50	FGHJKMNQUVXZ	1 = ₹75
Bank NIFTY	NBN	NSE	₹25 x Bank NIFTY	FGHJKMNQUVXZ	1 = ₹25
KOSPI 200	KOSPI	KRX	₩500,000 x KOSPI 200	HMUZ	1 = ₩500000
MSCI Taiwan	STW		$100 x SGX MSCI Taiwan	HMUZ	1 = $100

Figure 43: Contract specifications on Investing.com

7. USING OPTIONS IN A PORTFOLIO: MORE THAN ONE WAY OF WINNING

Creating models and visual representations to understand the moving parts of something can really help. For instance, I once worked at a company with a group of people who clearly disliked each other so much they could have been married. Their unifying bond was that they all disliked the company they worked for more than they disliked each other. Still, there was something wrong which needed to be understood. To try and get my head around this clinically-interesting situation, I borrowed my daughter's Sims computer game and set up a house – creating an avatar for each of the team members with a profile approximating to their personality. They were also given some toys like outdoor fireworks and a big TV to play with.

Within three minutes the team leader had set the outdoor fireworks off inside the house, killing one of the other team members in the process. With characteristic indifference, another team member on the way to the refrigerator stepped over the smouldering corpse of their colleague and emptied the icebox into their arms, taking the food with them up to bed. The others sat down in front of the over-sized television, only to perish in the flames. They were all dead within ten minutes of the start of the game. I realised then that this wasn't a sustainable work environment.

Sims is an example of what anthropologists call *speculative hunting* – the ability to think your way into the mind of your prey and predict their next move.[27] This is what we are going to do in this chapter: create visualisations for use when thinking about options contracts. To create the diagrams we are going to use, we can use a nifty spreadsheet, created by the good people at Robinson College of Business, which is freely available on the internet.[28]

To help you hunt down your prey – the markets – the following sections look at a number of ways you can use options, in combination with each other, to model what you think may happen in the days or weeks to come. The application is quite general; equities, indices, bonds, currencies and commodities can all be treated in this way. All you need is a view on the markets and the timescale over which your vision of endless hope might occur.

7.1 COMBINATIONS

So far we have only looked at buying or selling individual options: either the right to buy (calls) or the right to sell (puts) an underlying instrument. The BSM model of option pricing has also given us a picture of how the price of an option changes as the underlying commodity changes in price. Call options increase in value as the commodity's price rises above the strike price, while put options rise as the underlying's price falls below the strike price. For the owner, an option at expiration will either expire worthless (value $0) or have a value equal to the difference between the market price of the underlying (S) and the strike price (S_o). In mathematical terms, the maximum you can make is described like this:

---

27 *Born to Run*, Christopher McDougal, p.235.

28 www2.gsu.edu/~fncjtg/Fi8000/dnldpayoff.htm

Long call option value = $Max(0, S - S_0)$

Equation 26

Long put option value = $Max(0, S_0 - S)$

Equation 27

So, a call option with a strike price of $25 would have a value of $15, if the stock were trading at $40 at expiration. At or below $25, the value of the option will be zero.

If you are the seller (or writer, as the jargon has it) of an option then you have to turn the situation upside down. It is to your advantage if a call or put option expires valueless whereas you will lose money if it expires above (calls) or below (puts) the strike price. As a seller the maths looks like this:

Short call option value = $Min(0, S_0 - S)$

Equation 28

Short put option value = $Min(0, S - S_0)$

Equation 29

We can take this a step further and create a visual representation of an option pay-off diagram. Using the BSM model for a stock – Thales of Miletus PLC, trading at $24.6 with an annualised volatility of 35.7%, an interest rate of 1.5% and a one-year expiration – the European non-dividend-paying option profit/loss profiles would look like this:

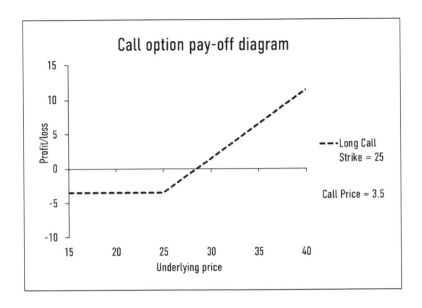

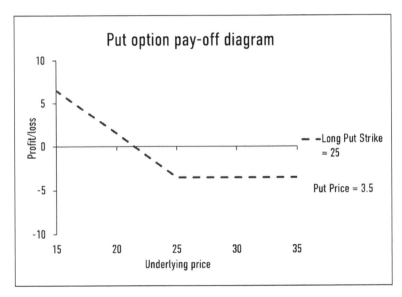

Figure 44: The pay-off diagrams of long call and put option positions

When the price of the underlying commodity is below $25, the value of the call option stays the same and the pay-off diagram line is flat. As soon as the market price exceeds $25, the profit starts to rise and the call option pay-off diagram takes on the characteristic hockey stick shape. The opposite is true of the put option.

Notice now that we are not talking exclusively about the *value* of the options; we want to know about the profit and loss profile for the investor – their pay-off. Buying options incurs a cost so, to break-even, the owner of an option must include the option premium in the pay-off diagram for a true picture of the profit and loss profile. This has the effect of shifting the whole pay-off graph downwards for options buyers. The break-even point is therefore:

Call option break-even = Stock price - Strike price + Option cost

Equation 30

Put option break-even = Strike price - Stock price - Option cost

Equation 31

The converse applies if you are the seller of an option; it has the effect of flipping the pay-off profile around the x-axis while rising to the extent of the option premium.

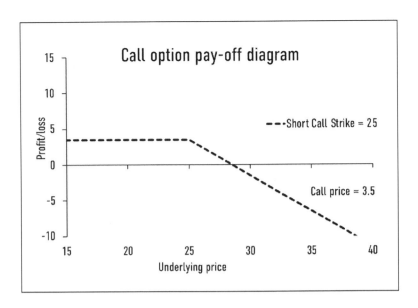

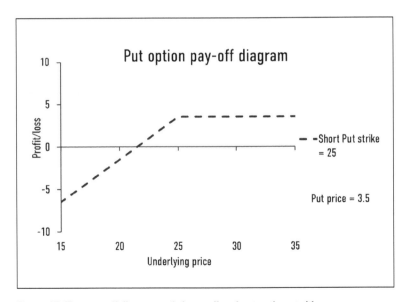

Figure 45: The pay-off diagrams of short call and put option positions

If you think about it for a moment, you could buy or sell options in any combination and, depending on how the market moves in the future, some will rise in value and some will fall in value. All the elements of options in combination: strike price, expiry date, buying/selling (long or short), as well as what flavour it is (put or call), lead to a huge variety of possibilities. These can all be represented as pay-off diagrams, and used to express our particular vision of the future for reasons of profit or to hedge against unwanted market volatility.

7.2   TO INFINITY AND BEYOND!

There are four basic shapes of options pay-off graphs:

- long a call option

- long a put option

- short a call option

- short a put option.

Make sure you understand the four pay-off diagrams in the previous section. These will form the basis of the discussions going forwards. One thing to note in all the examples of options: if you are *long* a call or a put and the market goes in your favour (up or down respectively) then your profit is unlimited. **Your loss is limited to the option premium.**

But if you are *short* a call, and the market moves against you, **your losses are unlimited**. If you are short a put option, your potential loss is equal to the difference between the strike price and zero, which is, effectively, the strike price. Finite losses versus infinite losses is why it is very dangerous to sell options **naked**, as they say, i.e., nothing backing it besides the figleaf of the contents of your bank account. Selling options is best done either in combination with an offsetting long option position or when you own the underlying commodity itself. In an investment career you will see people get away with naked option writing but in reality the clock is merely biding its time before they regret such a risky approach.

In the following sections we are going to look at the most popular option combinations.

7.3 THE STRADDLE

Brokers love straddles. If you ask a broker to price a straddle they will probably send an inappropriate present round after the transaction is completed, because it is just so expensive. A straddle consists of paying two premiums: simultaneously buying an at-the-money put and an at-the-money call with the same expiry date.

In the example below, an investor buys two one-year options with a strike price of 25 for a total premium of 7 points or 28.5% of the stock price value. Ouch! The pay-off diagram looks like this:

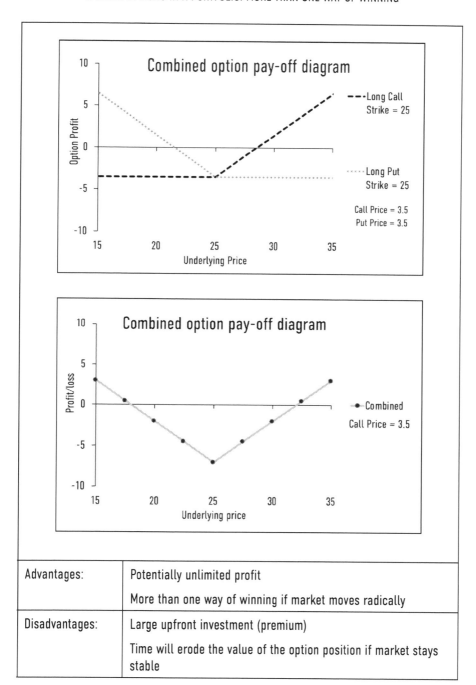

Advantages:	Potentially unlimited profit
	More than one way of winning if market moves radically
Disadvantages:	Large upfront investment (premium)
	Time will erode the value of the option position if market stays stable

Figure 46: The long straddle position

As long as the market moves significantly, over the remaining time to expiry of the options, the owner of the straddle is going to be a winner. If the market moves up, then the call becomes more valuable, but if the market moves down, the put becomes more valuable. In effect, you are betting on the market being volatile and directional but you just don't know which way it's going to go. This is known as 'buying volatility'. Financial assets *can* move radically in short periods of time and, as the owner of a straddle, you might think the high margin is a price worth paying to cover the uncertainty or make a profit.

There is another disadvantage of straddles. If the market doesn't move significantly then, as time goes by, the value of the combined option position will gradually fall away. If, for instance, the stock price at expiration is anywhere between 25 +/- 7 points, an investor will lose money because the premiums paid will exceed the profit. For straddle owners, time is your enemy.

You could, of course, take the opposite view and bet the markets aren't going to do very much in the coming months. In these circumstances, you could *sell* a straddle and take in the premium from the hapless and fretful person on the other side of the transaction. Over time, the option premium will decline as the time value of the option declines. The profit becomes the difference between the value of the premium you took in at the beginning and the value of the short straddle at expiration (which is hopefully nothing). In common parlance, you are **selling volatility** – since you are hoping the market doesn't move significantly but the buyer of the straddle does. It's quite a radical thing to do. If you work in a fund management company, walk into the private client department tomorrow morning and say "I've sold vol through an at-the-money straddle on yen/dollar at 118" and just watch the astonishment on their faces.

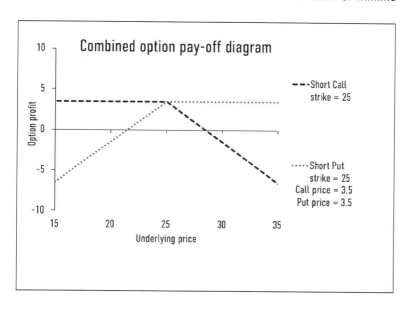

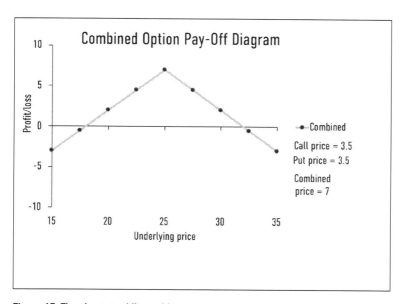

Figure 47: The short straddle position

7.4 THE STRANGLE

A strangle is similar to a straddle but both the put and call options are struck *out-of-the-money* (i.e., slightly either side of the current at-the-money price). Buying out-of-the-money options to create a long strangle is cheaper than a long straddle but it requires an even larger move in the underlying commodity to be profitable. Whereas the cost of the straddle in our example was 7 points, the cost of a strangle would be about 3.1 points – just by altering the strike prices from at-the-money to out-of-the-money. Again, as with the straddle position, time is your enemy; the pay-off will require a decisive move in the underlying commodity well before the expiration date.

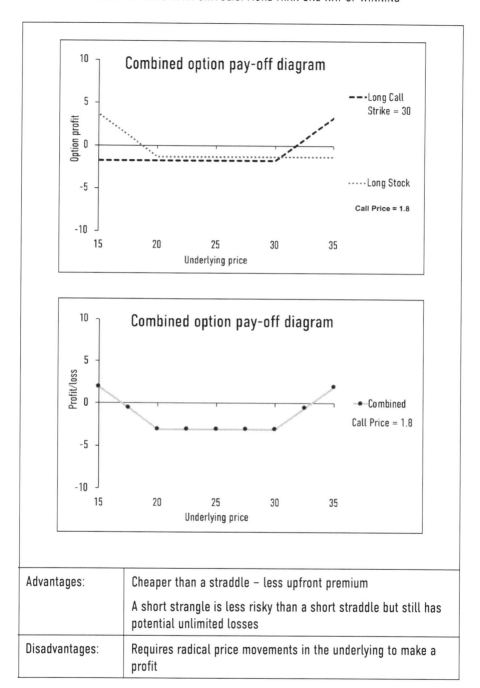

Advantages:	Cheaper than a straddle – less upfront premium
	A short strangle is less risky than a short straddle but still has potential unlimited losses
Disadvantages:	Requires radical price movements in the underlying to make a profit

Figure 48: The long strangle position

You could create a short strangle position, flipping the diagram upside down. As with a short straddle position, your losses are potentially unlimited and time is now your friend. But it is less risky than a short straddle position as the underlying price movement will have to be even more radical. Still, it remains a trade for the brave if not foolhardy.

7.5   SYNTHETIC FUTURE

To be absolutely honest, I've never seen anybody create a synthetic future. However, I wanted to put this idea in front of you because it illustrates how combining options together in imaginative ways can get you just about anything you want. Buying an at-the-money call, and selling an at-the-money put, creates a pay-off diagram which looks remarkably like owning the stock or owning a future. For this reason, it is known as owning a **synthetic future**. As before, every position has a mirror image so, if you wanted to create a synthetic short position to hedge a portfolio, you would simply sell the call option and buy the put option.

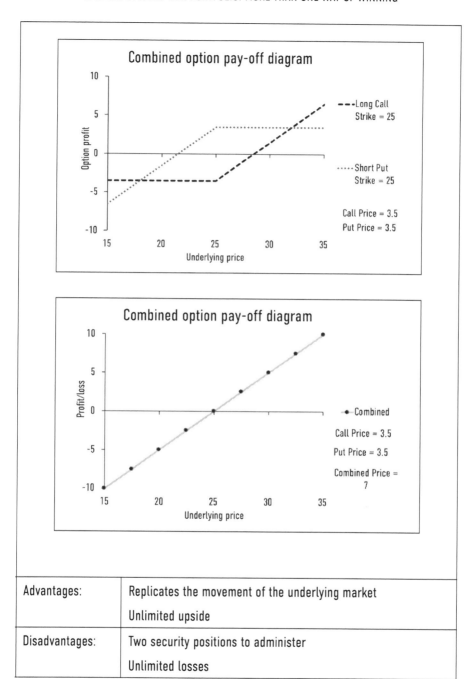

Figure 49: A synthetic future

The synthetic future introduces us to a useful way of thinking about combining derivatives together:

$$\text{Future} = \text{Call} - \text{Put}$$

Equation 32

You can rearrange this to:

$$\text{Call} = \text{Future} + \text{Put}$$

Equation 33

$$\text{Put} = \text{Call} - \text{Future}$$

Equation 34

More generally:

$$\text{Stock} + \text{Put} - \text{Call} = 0$$

Equation 35

Where o is really the discounted present value of the cash you would have to hold to buy the stock at expiration of the options. So,

$$\text{Stock} + \text{Put} - \text{Call} = \text{Strike price} \times e^{-rt}$$

Equation 36

where r is the deposit rate to expiration and t is the time to expiration of the options.

This is called the **put-call parity** and is the glue holding the derivatives market, the underlying markets and cash together. It's arguably one of the most important equations in modern finance although most people have never heard of it. Without it, the whole thing would fall apart because there would exist arbitrage opportunities to make riskless profits should anomalies persistently exist. Fortunately, there are people who spend their entire working days scouring the financial markets looking for anomalies violating the put-call parity principle. For instance, let's say call options were very expensive but you found a very cheap source of put options. You could sell call options to the market then create a cheap version of it through buying the puts and buying a future at the same time, thus locking in a profit. This is called **arbitrage** and, when performed on a massive enough scale, it has been known to generate equally massive profits. It also performs a useful function: the very act of buying or selling by arbitrageurs quickly brings the whole system back into equilibrium. They are like the small fish living around the teeth of sharks looking for left-over food. Arbitrage isn't really the stuff of day-to-day fund management but it is something to be aware of because it is an excellent way of understanding the relationship between all the elements of the financial system: assets, calls, puts, futures and cash.

7.6 COVERED CALL WRITING

Covered call writing must have been, and may yet be, the most profitable trade in derivatives there has ever been. In fact, it has been so profitable that a generation of MBA graduates pretty much drove it out of existence in the years between 1999 and 2007. It was, to be frank, easy money and as humans tend towards the easiest and most popular thing available you can understand why it got itself outlawed. Not because it was illegal but because too many people were doing it and it was basically traded out of existence. Fortunately, since then and the intervention of the Financial Crisis of 2008 it has returned.

Covered call writing is for people who own a stock or commodity and want to milk it for as much as possible while limiting their potential losses.

Using the nomenclature in the previous example:

Covered call = Future (underlying) - Call option

Equation 37

This strategy involves owning the underlying and selling (writing) an at-the-money call option for the same amount against it. Through the process of selling you take in a premium. The pay-off diagram looks like this:

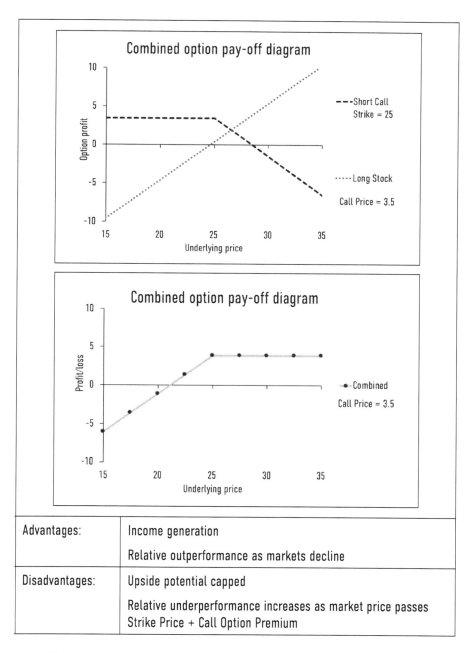

Advantages:	Income generation
	Relative outperformance as markets decline
Disadvantages:	Upside potential capped
	Relative underperformance increases as market price passes Strike Price + Call Option Premium

Figure 50: Covered call writing

On the face of it, I admit, this strategy doesn't quite live up to the billing I gave it in the introduction to this section. So let's think the possibilities through. If the market moves up to, say, $26 you will be *called* at expiration because the market price is above the call option strike price. To you, as the owner of the stock, the total return on the position will be:

$$\text{Total return} = \text{Proceeds from stock sale} + \text{Call option premium received}$$
$$= 25 + 3.5$$
$$= 28.5$$

Equation 38

In other words, this is better than just selling the stock to the market at $26 on the day of expiration. This trade will be profitable until the market price hits $28.5 on or before the expiration date. As the market moves up, your profit from the stock position becomes capped – you will definitely be called. You will now suffer an opportunity cost and a relative underperformance compared to a purely long stock position. As the market moves beyond strike price + call option premium, the underperformance intensifies. If you are thinking about absolute returns, you might not mind this, but if you are competing against an index you are now at a disadvantage.

Now let's imagine the market moves down to $20. In this case, you will not be called by the option owner at expiration because they will be able to buy the stock cheaper in the market. Your total return would be:

Total return = Proceeds from stock sale + Call option
premium received
$$= 15 + 3.5$$
$$= \$18.5$$

You have made a loss but you have outperformed the market to the extent of the option premium. You have performed better compared to just blindly owning the stock and not having a view on future movements. However, the market has gone down and you will have made an absolute loss.

There is also an important principle at stake here: **option premium gathered in this way is classified in accounting terms as income and can be distributed to investors as a dividend**. If you are managing an income fund, or the portfolio of a client whose goal is income rather than capital gains, making directional views of this sort is one way of boosting income – if you get it right.

7.7   IT CAN BE TERRIBLY COLD WHEN YOU ARE NAKED...

There really are things called naked positions in the derivatives markets. They are also referred to as **uncovered** positions. As you can see in the pay-off diagrams below, when you are short a put or short a call option, your losses can be substantial.

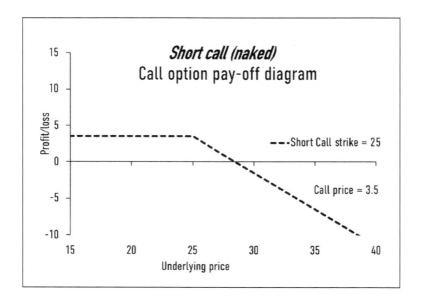

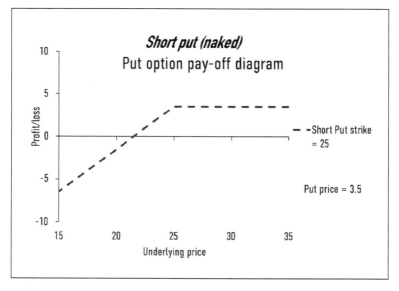

Figure 51: Pay-off graphs for naked options

Selling uncovered options has got more fund managers into trouble than anything else I can think of. Sometimes an uncovered position has been entered into on purpose, as part of a market strategy, but, more often than not, it has been because, somewhere down the line, someone got the wrong message and sold when they should have bought, resulting in an accidental short position. This is where Cowley's Second Law of Finance comes in:

'Accidental profits are always small but accidental losses are always large.'

Don't forget you are writing (selling) options on something you don't own in your portfolio so one day you may have to fund the actions of the person exercising their rights. If you sell a call option, your best hope is that, at expiration, the stock price is below the strike price. The other side of the trade won't call stock away from you because they can buy it for less in the market. You will realise a profit ($3.5 in our example) from selling a valueless option.

If the stock price goes to $100, however, the call option owner will exercise their rights and you will have to go and buy the stock in the market. Your total cost will be:

$$\text{Total cost} = \text{Cost of stock} + \text{Call option premium received}$$
$$= -100 + 3.5$$
$$= -\$96.5$$

If your total portfolio is only worth $90 in cash terms, you are now bust.

Now let's consider a naked put option. This time you sell the put at a strike of $25 and take in a premium of $3.5. At expiration, the stock has fallen to $1. The owner of the put option will want to sell the stock to you at the strike price of $25, so your total return will look like this:

$$\text{Total return} = \text{Cost of stock} + \text{Put option premium received}$$
$$= -25 + 3.5$$
$$= -\$21.5$$

Equation 39

Again, you will make a substantial loss (24%) on your $90 fund. Your investors won't be happy.

These two examples illustrate why selling naked call options is so dangerous. You can lose very substantial amounts of money if you do this – either knowingly or unknowingly (by accidentally selling when you should be buying) – and the underlying commodity moves against you.

7.8 VOLATILITY

The volatility of markets is one of the main determinants of whether investors think options are cheap or expensive. The more volatile the markets are, the more uncertain the result at expiration and the more expensive the options will be. In less volatile markets, where the risk of bad outcomes are perceived to be lower, options will be cheaper.

There are two types of volatility that derivatives investors talk about:

- implied volatility
- historical volatility.

Historical volatility is the standard deviation of prices. It is a mathematically-calculated value derived from an historical price series. You can't really argue with it. However, implied volatility is an altogether different idea. By turning the BSM equation upside down, you start with market price and work backwards to calculate what volatility would justify the observed price. In this way, you can start the process of thinking about whether you should be buying or selling options: is the implied volatility higher or lower than recent history? If you are fortunate enough to have access to a system like Bloomberg, this is where the Historical Volitility Graph (HVG) screen comes into its own; it can give you a sense of perspective. Let's use an example: the current S&P 500 futures contract. Type SPA Comdty HVG <GO> and you will see something like this:

Figure 52: Historical price volatility (six months daily) of an S&P 500 futures contract (Source: Bloomberg)

This shows the historical volatility of the futures contract, calculated using data from the past ten, 30 and 90 days. As you can see from the graph, back in October 2008 things were pretty uncertain (volatility was high) but things have calmed down a lot since then. Even the longer-term volatility is trending down. But if we change the value in the Period field to One Year Daily, we get a different perspective.

Figure 53: Historical price volatility (one year daily) of an S&P 500 futures contract (Source: Bloomberg)

From this example you can see that things have calmed down but the annualised volatility, at close to 40%, is still twice as high it was a year ago when it was 'only' 20% per annum. The important point here is: **when assessing market situations make sure you take into account both long-term and short-term perspectives before making a judgment**.

In the top right of the HVG screen you can see two fields: Ivol Call and Ivol Put. These stand for the implied volatility on puts and calls.

Change the Ivol Call tab to Yes and zero out the historical data by unchecking the box to left. Change the Period back to Six Months Daily. You will now see the observed volatility built into prices of call options in the past six months. Again, we can see option volatility has come down a lot in the period which might lead you to think options are cheap. But, again, perspective is our friend. Change the Period tab to One Year Daily and you get a very different picture. Now we can see the harsh reality: implied option volatility has merely fallen from *astonishingly high to amazingly high.*

Figure 54: Implied option volatility (Source: Bloomberg)

In these circumstances, you might be tempted to just shut down your Bloomberg and go home. But the derivatives markets don't let you off so lightly. What is possible is only limited by your own imagination – there is *always* something you can do.

For every non-purchase there is a possible sale; for every sideways market there is a combination option strategy someone could buy from you; for every uncertainty there is a position you could take expressing a change in the market direction.

Could you, for instance, be tempted to sell covered calls to take advantage of these high prices in the options market? There is a market judgment to be made here about the extent to which the markets have calmed down or will calm down going forwards. This could make covered call writing potentially very profitable for an income-hungry portfolio.

In the derivatives markets, every cloud really does have a silver lining.

7.9 CONCLUSION

Sir Martin Frobisher is one of my favourite figures in history. In the 16th century, Frobisher explored the arctic region of Canada and discovered the highest grade of gold ore the world had ever seen. So rich was it, it twinkled a yellow lustre in a way normal gold ore doesn't. Dutifully, he loaded 200 tons of the stuff onto his comically small boat and took it back to England where everyone agreed it was worth an astonishing £5.20 a ton.

Emboldened by his discovery, Frobisher returned to Canada, this time transporting 1,350 tons of the gold ore back to England. After several years of smelting, and much head-scratching, it was realised that the 'gold ore' was worthless iron pyrites. Realising metallurgy wasn't his strong point, Frobisher turned his hand to plundering French ships (you could say he became an *iron pirate*) and earned a knighthood for his exploits against the Spanish Armada in 1588. But if the term 'fool's gold' didn't exist before Sir Martin Frobisher, then it most certainly did after him.

Frobisher teaches us a useful lesson we can use in the markets. You take a view, you make your bets and you live with the consequences. What Sir Martin didn't give himself was an insurance policy against the idea of him being wrong. The result was therefore black or white, right or wrong, lavish riches or road ballast. There wasn't too much of a grey area, besides Sir Martin's hair shortly after being told he'd got it wrong – again.

During the course of this chapter, we have learned that life doesn't have to be like this. We've considered how you can use derivatives in a portfolio – by combining them with other derivatives – to give you a chance of winning under a range of circumstances, not just one. However, derivatives *per se* aren't some kind of magic bullet. For a derivatives strategy to work, you will need a view of what the world will be like in the days or months ahead.

This is a critical point. Once you have come to a conclusion about what you think, then the solutions are pretty trivial. The derivatives market will most likely be able to come up with a single security or combination of them to express your view. Excitingly, if you *can* form a view, it will probably put you in the top 10% of fund managers in the world.

8. THE MECHANICS OF DERIVATIVES: LIVING ON THE MARGIN

Until recently, the idea that a bank could go bust had been relegated to shaky black-and-white movies of distraught investors standing on window ledges in 1929. In 2008, we rediscovered banks aren't the safe, boring institutions we thought they were. What's more, there is the distinct possibility one or more of these banks won't be around to honour their commitments when the next financial crisis hits. Hell, the next big thing could be a developed-world country going bust.

So, if you are trading a forward agreement, or any other over-the-counter (OTC) agreement, with one of these wobbly mathematical jellies, counterparty risk isn't just a fanciful theoretical consideration but something you need to take very seriously. In this chapter, we are going to look at how the derivatives markets are organised in order to reduce the risk the other side of your trade won't be around to pay up, when the time comes.

8.1 IT'S A FAIR EXCHANGE...

The derivatives markets are organised into **exchanges**. Members of the exchange come together to buy and sell standardised contracts on behalf of their clients. The bargains struck are cleared (settled) through a central body, passing money between accounts registering the profit and loss of clients. Any one bargain could contain many trades split between separate counterparties. For example, selling 100 futures contracts could consist of any combination of trades (10, 1, 13, 25, etc.) each with a different buyer – all you can see is that you sold 100 contracts. This has the effect of smearing out risk around the system. This is a very important property of derivatives traded on centralised exchanges.

Of course, to trade on the exchange you will need a broker to pass your trades to the market. Although it's beyond the scope of this book, it's enough to say that getting access to the derivatives markets requires some documentation proving your creditworthiness and giving an indication that you know what you are doing. But, in essence, opening a derivatives account with a broker is no different to opening any other account to trade stocks and bonds. If you want to do it as a private investor, you can complete the process online in just a few minutes. If you are an institution, the paperwork is a little more onerous as you are acting for client money under an umbrella agreement.

Schematically, the organisation of the market looks like this:

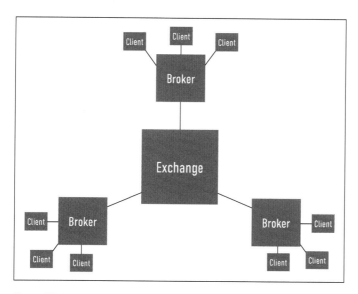

Figure 55: The role of a derivatives exchange

When you establish a futures position, you have to stump up some cash just to get going. The percentage of the notional position you have to put up is a function of the specific contract being traded, and how risky a client you are perceived to be. Those classified as *speculators* have to put up more than, for example, an enormous pension fund. The amount of money you have to hand over is called the **initial margin**.

Each day, each second even, the market is going to move up and down and you will make or lose money on the position. In the case of exchange-traded futures, if a loss-making position starts to accumulate you may be asked to add money to your account. This happens when you hit a level called the **maintenance margin**. This is where the phrase **margin call** comes from; someone may literally call and ask you to transfer more money to cover your accumulating losses. The difference between the maintenance margin and the initial margin, called the **variation margin,** is the amount you will need to add to your account.[29] If you make a profit, it is credited to your account in a notional form but it is unwise to take it out before the transaction is complete.

The amount of money a futures contract covers is dependent upon the individual contract. Bond futures can have a nominal of $100,000, for instance. To cover $1,000,000 you would need ten contracts (1,000,000/100,000). Stock index futures are valued per index point. So, for instance, an S&P 500 stock index future is valued at $250 per point and the initial margin is a fixed percentage of the value of the futures position.

To illustrate this, let's use an index future on the S&P 500 index and price it using the continuous compounding method. The calculation looks very similar to previous examples: it is a three-month future, the current index level is 2,700, there is an interest rate and an assumed dividend yield. All the things you should by now expect when valuing a futures contract. The new factors we have introduced are:

- the value of each index point of the future is $250

- the number of contracts we have purchased is 10

- the initial margin is 4% of the nominal value.

From this, we can calculate all we need to know about the position:

- the theoretical value of the future

- the total value of the futures position

- the initial margin

- the profit and loss given today's market level of the futures contract.

	A	B
1	Index Level	2,700
2	Time (Years)	0.25
3	Deposit Rate (annualised)	3.00%
4	Dividend Yield (annualised)	1.70%
5	Interest Rate Difference	1.30%
6	Time Weighted Interest Rate Difference	0.33%
7	Theoretical Futures Price	2,709
8	Value of an Index Point	250
9	Value of One Future	677,197
10	Number of Futures Purchased	10
11	Total Value of Position	6,771,973
12	Initial Margin @ 4%	270,879
13	Intital Futures Price	2,709
14	Profit or (Loss)	0

	A	B
1	Index Level	2700
2	Time (Years)	0.25
3	Deposit Rate (annualised)	0.03
4	Dividend Yield (annualised)	0.017
5	Interest Rate Difference	=B3-B4
6	Time Weighted Interest Rate Difference	=B5*B2
7	Theoretical Futures Price	=B1*EXP(B6)
8	Value of an Index Point	250
9	Value of One Future	=B8*B7
10	Number of Futures Purchased	10
11	Total Value of Position	=B10*B9
12	Initial Margin @ 4%	=B11*0.04
13	Intital Futures Price	2708.78927483522
14	Profit or (Loss)	=(B7-B13)*B10*B8

Figure 56: Calculating margin requirements

So, given the information we know, the theoretical value of the future is 2,709 making the value of one contract $677,197 (2,709 × $250). Buying ten contracts will cover ten times this amount and, at 4% initial margin, we have to put up $270,879 (4% × $6,771,973).

When the deal is struck there is no variation in the profit and loss of the position because nothing has changed. But after a single day, or even a couple of minutes, something will have happened. The nature of restless, twitching markets is to constantly create winners and losers in the process known as **price discovery** – the elusive metastable equilibrium point where all known information and opinion has been expressed through the medium of trade.

Let's imagine two scenarios: the market has risen to 2,750 and fallen to 2,650. To find out what happens to our profit and loss account, change the Index Level value in cell B1.

	A	B
1	Index Level	2,750
2	Time (Years)	0.25
3	Deposit Rate (annualised)	3.00%
4	Dividend Yield (annualised)	1.70%
5	Interest Rate Difference	1.30%
6	Time Weighted Interest Rate Difference	0.33%
7	Theoretical Futures Price	2,759
8	Value of an Index Point	250
9	Value of One Future	689,738
10	Number of Futures Purchased	10
11	Total Value of Position	6,897,380
12	Initial Margin @ 4%	275,895
13	Intital Futures Price	2,709
14	Profit or (Loss)	125,407

	A	B
1	Index Level	2,650
2	Time (Years)	0.25
3	Deposit Rate (annualised)	3.00%
4	Dividend Yield (annualised)	1.70%
5	Interest Rate Difference	1.30%
6	Time Weighted Interest Rate Difference	0.33%
7	Theoretical Futures Price	2,659
8	Value of an Index Point	250
9	Value of One Future	664,657
10	Number of Futures Purchased	10
11	Total Value of Position	6,646,566
12	Initial Margin @ 4%	265,863
13	Intital Futures Price	2,709
14	Profit or (Loss)	(125,407)

Figure 57: Loss-making positions can lead to a margin call

If the market moves up to 2,750, profits are accrued to your account (+$125,407). But if the market moves down to 2,650 then losses accrue (-$125,407) to your account. It will depend on the arrangements you have with your broker but, as the market hits 2,650, you may have breached your maintenance margin line – because nearly half of your

$270,000 initial margin just evaporated. You should be expecting your mobile to ring anytime now for variation margin.

In reality, most people post a little more initial margin than necessary to avoid tiresome margin calls (the broker will invest the money in some ultra-safe money market instrument like a government Treasury bill). Nevertheless, the process known as **mark-to-market** – when client accounts are valued at the end of each day – is a watershed moment. It can also be a frightening experience for some people. So if your idea of hell is pineapple in coleslaw, you probably aren't cut out for futures trading.

8.2   A WORD ON TECHNOLOGY

If you are a professional investor and a Bloomberg user, there is a quick way of finding out what is going on in the derivatives markets. You can find the popular spot prices and exchange-traded contracts on a single screen, which you can watch for hours on end while pretending to be working (this has been my habit from time to time).

For instance, the Commodities Research Bureau (CRB) publishes live spot prices for popular commodities. To access this Bloomberg screen, press CRB <GO> and instantly you will see a screen similar to the example below. It is a summary of real-time commodity prices for things like gold, wheat and lean hogs.

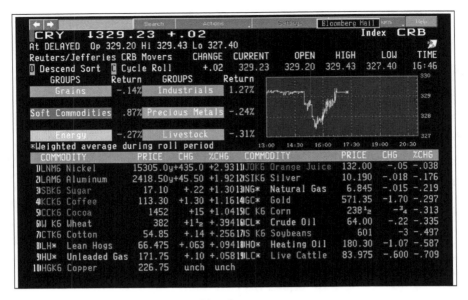

Figure 58: CRB spot commodity prices in Bloomberg

The breadth and depth of the derivatives markets available on Bloomberg can be a little daunting at times. To save you a lot of time here is a summary of the main ones:

Exchange/ markets	Bloomberg ticker	Description	Commodities covered
Commodities	CRB <GO>	Major commodity indices	Energy, agriculture, metals
Metals	METL <GO>	Spot and three-month forward metals	Precious metals, base metals, steel
Energy	LFP <GO>	Oil, gasoil and natural gas	Brent crude, Middle East sour, gasoil, natural gas
Crops	CRPM <GO>	Grown commodities	Dairy, livestock, ethanol, grain, rubber, textiles, tropical products
Stock markets	WEIF <GO>	Equity futures	North/Latin America, Europe/Africa, Asia/Pacific equity markets
Bond markets	WBF <GO>	Global government bond futures	North/Latin America, Europe/Africa, Asia/Pacific government bond futures along the yield curve where available
Interest rates	WIR <GO>	One and three-month money market futures	North/Latin America, Europe/Africa, Asia/Pacific exchanges
Currencies	CEM 5 <GO>	Currency futures exchanges	North America, South America, Europe, Pacific Rim, Africa and Middle East currency and commodity exchanges

Figure 59: Bloomberg ticker codes for the main derivatives markets

For those private investors who don't have the $2,000[30] it costs each month for a Bloomberg terminal, here are some internet resources you might like to play with (I have no affiliation with these sites). The website danielstrading.com provides a futures position calculator.[31] This and other sites will also give you useful information on margin requirements.[32]

Let's look at a few examples using the danielstrading.com calculator.

Below, I've input a version of the S&P index futures called the E-mini along with the Comex gold future. The drop-down menu allows you to see the details of the contract, how much the contract is worth per point of movement, and the minimum price movement (tick size). I've also input some dummy trades to show what happens to the profit and loss.

Futures Market

Select a Futures Market

E-mini S&P 500 (ES) - Globex	▾

E-mini S&P 500 (ES) - Globex	
Price Format Example	1120.00
Contract Size	$50 x index value
Minimum Tick Fluctuation/Value	0.25 / $12.50
Point Value	1.00 / $50.00
Margin Requirements	Margin
Delivery Months	H, M, U, Z
Trading Hours	Hours
Exchange	CME
Delivery Month Symbol Key	Jan=F, Feb=G, Mar=H, Apr=J, May=K, Jun=M, Jul=N, Aug=Q, Sep=U, Oct=V, Nov=X, Dec=Z

Enter Price Information and Number of Futures Contracts

Bullish		
Entry Price (Buy)	Exit Price (Sell)	Number of contracts
1120	1250	10
Profit or Loss (Ticks)	Profit or Loss (Points)	Profit or Loss (USD$)
5200.00	1300.00	$65000.00

30 qz.com/84961/this-is-how-much-a-bloomberg-terminal-costs
31 www.danielstrading.com/trading-resources/futures-calculator
32 bportal.gainfutures.com/margins?WLID=74&_
     ga=2.52150825.1009883579.1516186916-2101344714.1516186916

Figure 60: Internet resources like danielstrading.com offer position monitoring

In this example, the S&P 500 index has moved up to 1,250 from 1,120 so the ten-contract position has generated a profit of $65,000 (130 × $50 × 10). I also bought ten Comex gold contracts at $1,050 which have fallen to $1,025 creating a loss of -$25,000 (25 × $10 × 10). Swings and roundabouts as they say.

You could call this the 'it is what it is' approach because you need little or no understanding of *how* the fair value of a future is derived – you can simply treat the contracts as instruments relentlessly moving up and down in price, each fraction giving rise to the winning or losing of money. While I am not advocating it, there are a remarkable number of people who do spend their days pursuing intraday profits like this; treating the derivatives markets as they would any other betting game. If you want to do this, sites like Investing.com offer free real-time prices (as well as the opportunity to open a trading account).

Investing.com   Search the website...

Real Time Streaming Futures Quotes (CFDs)

Price | Performance | Technical | Specification | Candlestick Patterns   ⬇ Download Data

Index	Month	Last	High	Low	Chg.	Chg. %	Time
Dow 30	Dec 18	24,790.0	24,860.0	24,574.0	+174.0	+0.71%	08:05:51
S&P 500	Dec 18	2,685.25	2,692.50	2,659.00	+21.00	+0.79%	08:05:50
Nasdaq	Dec 18	6,929.25	6,966.00	6,817.75	+93.00	+1.36%	08:05:51
SmallCap 2000	Dec 18	1,481.8	1,486.7	1,470.2	+12.0	+0.82%	08:05:52
S&P 500 VIX	Nov 18	20.40	20.88	20.17	-0.23	-1.09%	08:05:53
DAX	Dec 18	11,215.5	11,257.5	11,046.5	+39.0	+0.35%	08:05:52
CAC 40	Nov 18	5,009.2	5,027.5	4,910.5	+59.7	+1.21%	08:05:52
FTSE 100	Dec 18	6,935.8	6,956.0	6,861.0	-5.2	-0.07%	08:05:52
Euro Stoxx 50	Dec 18	3,140.0	3,150.0	3,095.0	+19.0	+0.61%	08:05:51
FTSE MIB	Dec 18	18,742.50	18,762.50	18,362.50	+303.50	+1.65%	08:05:50
SMI	Dec 18	8,623.0	8,691.0	8,579.0	-96.0	-1.10%	08:05:51
IBEX 35	Nov 18	8,737.0	8,773.0	8,603.5	+67.4	+0.78%	08:05:52
ATX	Dec 18	3,073.0	3,073.0	3,030.0	+23.5	+0.77%	07:01:00
WIG20	Dec 18	2,133.50	2,144.50	2,116.50	-14.50	-0.68%	08:03:44
AEX	Nov 18	509.93	511.81	501.68	+4.01	+0.79%	08:05:52
BUX	Dec 18	36,545	36,715	36,060	+95	+0.26%	07:54:48
RTS	Dec 18	111,335	112,040	110,405	-1075	-0.96%	08:05:53
OBX	Nov 18	810.15	811.35	793.25	+2.04	+0.25%	08:05:47
OMXS30	Nov 18	1,494.38	1,506.50	1,482.88	-3.37	-0.23%	08:05:52
Greece 20	Nov 18	1,672.75	1,674.00	1,635.00	+36.00	+2.20%	24/10
IBovespa	Dec 18	84,375	84,455	84,268	+756	+0.90%	08:05:51
Nikkei 225	Dec 18	21,545.0	21,598.0	21,197.5	+275.0	+1.29%	08:05:51
TOPIX	Dec 18	1,619.00	1,622.25	1,595.75	-5.25	-0.32%	08:05:53
Hang Seng	Oct 18	24,936.5	25,026.0	24,601.5	+40.5	+0.16%	08:05:53
China H-Shares	Oct 18	10,170.5	10,195.5	9,977.0	-48.5	-0.47%	04:14:55
CSI 300	Oct 18	3,191.60	3,256.80	3,174.00	+11.00	+0.35%	24/10
China A50	Oct 18	11,364.0	11,389.0	11,029.0	+44.0	+0.39%	08:05:27
S&P/ASX 200	Dec 18	5,666.5	5,728.5	5,616.5	-33.0	-0.58%	08:05:44
Singapore MSCI	Oct 18	341.05	343.25	338.85	-3.60	-1.04%	08:05:51
Nifty 50	Oct 18	10,165.25	10,211.75	10,118.30	-63.30	-0.62%	08:05:52
Bank NIFTY	Nov 18	25,007.55	25,097.80	24,820.00	-195.80	-0.78%	05:59:00
KOSPI 200	Dec 18	266.1	267.8	263.8	-6.0	-2.21%	01:00:00
MSCI Taiwan	Oct 18	357.05	358.70	352.00	-2.45	-0.68%	08:05:05

Figure 61: A typical screen showing real-time price changes (Source: Investing.com)

8.3   CONCLUSION

The derivatives markets are a place you can let your imagination go wild. Nothing seems to be off-limits. To the list of available contracts we really should add futures on Bitcoin, the blockchain-based cryptocurrency. The launch of Bitcoin futures, in December 2017, was hailed as a major step forwards in the process of including electrocurrencies into mainstream investment.[33] To say this particular future lies at the highly-speculative end of a spectrum of speculation is no understatement. Bitcoin futures can move 20% in a day purely on supply and demand perceptions and, more worryingly, market chatter.[34] But it just goes to show that if you can define something which has a price attached to it, someone will be prepared to create a derivative for it. Major derivatives groups like CME and CBOE have Bitcoin futures trading with their names on them. If you are interested, the Commodities Futures Trading Commission has launched an online information portal to educate the public on digital commodities.[35]

There are no free lunches in the financial markets (especially since the compliance department clamped down on them). But there aren't many restaurants where you can order a meal with a small downpayment and, if you don't like it, only pay for what you ate or, if it's really good, sell the meal to the highest bidder. This is the futures markets in a nutshell.

---

33 www.independent.co.uk/news/business/news/bitcoin-futures-launch-cme-group-chicago-cryptocurrency-mainstream-trading-a8116656.html

34 www.cnbc.com/2018/01/16/bitcoin-price-slips-to-its-lowest-level-in-six-weeks.html

35 www.coindesk.com/cftc-launches-online-resources-bitcoin-investors

During the course of this section, you should have understood the following:

- counterparty risk is a very real danger

- using futures can reduce counterparty risk

- to enter into a derivatives contract you will have to put up a fraction of the notional value of the trade

- subsequent price movements will result in profits and losses which may require additional funds to be supplied.

8.4 OUTRO

Even Karl Marx acknowledged communism couldn't really work anywhere except on a piece of paper because, without a competitive engine at the centre of an economy driving it forwards, society wouldn't go anywhere of its own volition. As far as Marxism was concerned, theory was better than reality. You could argue that lifting communism off the written page, and its subsequent failure, laid the way for the unfettered capitalism which has become the new normal in the world (rightly or wrongly). The spread of capitalism and democracy has turned human beings into the most successful species on the planet (besides the insects – they have been *way* more successful). It has never been a better time to be alive if you are a human being; we live longer, are better educated, better fed, less in poverty and have lower infant mortality rates than ever before in human history.

Despite the naysayers, there is nothing intrinsically wrong with the core activity of the capitalist system: people with ideas raise money to create companies. In turn, the new companies create jobs and services satisfying the needs of a functioning and open democratic society. Tired and exhausted entrepreneurs live in big houses and swagger around their local golf clubs of a weekend while bright-eyed employees live in more modest houses and go fishing, have pensions, and sleep quietly in their beds at night because they don't carry the worries their bosses are burdened with. Everyone is happy.

In the process of turning ideas into big houses, there are links in the chain where people can sell services. There are investment banks who have the contacts to raise capital, in the form of shares and bonds, to create the companies; investment managers buy and sell the shares and bonds for their clients in a zero-sum game which transfers money around the system; consultants advise clients which fund managers are best at managing money or, rather, least-worst at transferring it to another fund manager; pension funds, which are created by companies for their employees, are managed by the same fund managers and advised by the same consultants. An enormous circular dependency culture is created between innovation, job creation and wealth management. At every intervening point in the process, intermediaries can enrich themselves by taking 0.01% of massive amounts of money in commission and fees. The rewards for fund managers and service providers can look disproportionate compared to, say, the average nurse's salary mainly because they are.

As time has progressed, competition for business and the creation of league tables of fund manager performance have blown away the cobwebs from this opaque and cosy cartel. This new competitive environment has coincided with a rapid decline in the cost of using derivatives, while technology to manage their administration has become widely adopted. Derivatives are no longer the preserve of a few geeks who were lifted out of university science and engineering departments two decades ago. Financial haute couture has hit the high street.

The passage of time has also helped in the process of education. Both regulators and fledgling fund managers, with qualifications like the Chartered Financial Analyst (CFA) certificate (which includes a derivatives module), are rising through the management ranks. A new generation is now emerging who are both comfortable and familiar with the theoretical aspects of derivatives. This generation is quite rightly demanding modern investment managers start using derivatives in their working lives as a matter of course, rather than as some eccentric exception. What's more, as with the price of any commodity, mass usage and more players have driven the cost of derivatives down. This has created savings for fund managers which can be passed on to the end-user (i.e., the general public).

My final word on this subject, as a triple-A rated fund manager with thirty years of commercial experience behind him, is this. There are really only two elements to being a professional fund manager you need to remember: perform and sell. Perform for your existing clients and sell your skills to new ones. From this, four permutations for your professional life emerge:

- If you are not performing but still selling, then you are all right.

- If you are performing but not selling, you are also all right.

- If you are both performing and selling, then you get to live in a big house.

- If you are neither performing nor selling, you should go and get a black bin liner to put your possessions in – I'll see you down the pub for commiserations.

Your job, going forwards, is to stay within the first three possibilities. Using derivatives could just help.